PANCHAYATI RAJ INSTITUTIONS
ISSUES AND CHALLENGES

PANCHAYATI RAJ INSTITUTIONS

ISSUES AND CHALLENGES

By

Rajib Lochan Panigrahy

DISCOVERY PUBLISHING HOUSE

NEW DELHI-110002

First Published-2007
Reprinted-2014
ISBN 978-81-8356-197-6

Published by

DISCOVERY PUBLISHING HOUSE
4831/24, Ansari Road, Prahlad Street,
Darya Ganj, New Delhi-110002 (India)
Phone: 23279245 • Fax: 91-11-23253475
E-mail: dphbooks@rediffmail.com
dphtemp@indiatimes.com

Printed at:

Shree Balaji Art Press

Editorial

Panchayati Raj Institutions (PRIs) are derived form the community participation of rural inhabitants for their self-governance. To rule their own community or to manage themselves. Panchayats have been formed. In panchayats few people nominated by them from them to give decisions and others obey their words. They will sit on a high place or in village common *varandaha* or community home with a meeting of village people which is now named as *Gram Sabha* or *Palli Sabha*. From that panchayat governance, higher governments have been developed and it became lower level, others ruling it. It is such type of government nd only government which can cope and continue without others assistance and also that will be for development of the community. The higher governments achieving their goal with the help of PRIs. When some emergencies appears in Panchayats, no government reaches, there no assistance come to that, the rural self-reliant people manage that after the emergencies managed others reaching there and makes propaganda that they helped the needy. There are many resources in rural areas and no facilities of government reaching there. So, where is the development of the economy like India. Only the rural mass and PRIs are utilised by politicians, mediators, fants, MP, MLAs at the time of election by announcing many commitments as *Rama Rajya* is no distant form them. After election completes villages are as it is before and no commitment becomes true. All the policies of government is not utilising properly and are only in policies.

Editor

Contents

1

Role of Panchayati Raj Institutions in the Rural Development: A Management Study

Dr. Sudhansu Sekhar Nayak*
Dr. Anil Kumar Sahu**

Introduction

Orissa is one of the few states in the post-independent period to take up the Panchayati Raj as its main fulcrum of rural administration - Orissa Grama Panchayat Act, was enacted in the year 1948. Subsequently, in the year 1961, 3-tier system of Panchayati Raj Institutions was introduced in Orissa. Over the past 58 years, Panchayati Raj Institutions have emerged as the powerful institutions in bringing about rapid and sustainable development and socio-economic transformation in rural Orissa. It has an integrated prospective towards improving the quality of lives of rural people and ensuring equity and effective people's participation. Seventy-third amendment of the Constitution has conferred constitutional status to Panchayati Raj Institutions (PRIs). The provisions of Panchayats Act aims at empowering Panchayati Raj Institutions in scheduled areas for economic development and social justice. In the year 2002, election to 3-tier of Panchayati Raj Institutions held in conformity with 73rd Amendment. The prime objectives of the three-tier Panchayati Raj system are to eradicate poverty, uplift the living standard of people in the rural areas, bring about a healthy society by

* Lecturer in Commerce, R.N. College, Dura, Berhampur-10, Ganjam (Orissa).

** Reader in MBA, Berhampur University, Bhanja Bihar (Orissa).

creating awareness for hygiene, sanitation and eradication of illiteracy. At present 1,00,862 elected representatives of 30 Zilla Parishads, 314 Panchayat Samities and 6,234 Gram Panchayats are getting the opportunity to participate in the governance of PRIs.

Rural development is the main pillar of state development. Rural Orissa has lagged behind in development because of many historical reasons. The thrust of policies and programmes of Panchayati Raj Department is on all round economic development and social justice through empowerment. The activities of PR Department can be classified into following categories:

- Poverty Amelioration programme.
- Strengthening PRIs.
- Providing Basic Services.

Orissa's poverty is an enigma for planners and administrators. This programme has four major components and these are:

- Wage-employment programme.
- Self-employment programme.
- Housing for the poor.
- Development of Rural Infrastructure.
- Marketing initiative through ORMAS.

The above-mentioned objectives are achieved through SGRY, SGSY, IAY, PMGY, Operation Black-board, Rural Connectivity Programme, etc.

Scope and Objective of the Study

In this paper we have tried our best to highlight the role played by the Panchayati Raj Institutions (PRIs) for the rural development in Southern Orissa. It consists of eight districts, namely, Ganjam, Gajapati, Koraput, Malkangiri, Nawarangpur, Rayagada, Boudh and Knadhalmal. For the purpose of our study, we have taken up only one scheme that is Swarnajayanti Gram Swarojagar Yojana, briefly known as SGSY scheme during the year 2003-04 and only secondary data are taken into consideration. So, all limitations of the secondary data are found in this study.

About Swarnajayanti Gram Swarojagar Yojana (SGSY)

The Swarnajayanti Gram Swarojagar Yojana (SGSY) scheme was launched with effect from 1st April, 1999 throughout the rural areas of the country. This scheme have been restructured into a single self-employment programme by amalgamation of six schemes, i.e.:

- Integrated Rural Development Programme (IRDP)
- Training of Rural Youths for Self-employment (TRYSEM),
- Development of Women and Children in Rural Area (DWCRA),
- Supply of Improved Tool-kits to Rural Artisans (SITRA),
- Ganga Kalyan Yojana (GKY),
- Million Well Schemes (MWS).

To provide financial credit especially to rural poor like SC, ST, OBC, women and disabled.

The SGSY is conceived as a holistic programme of micro enterprises covering all aspects of self-employment which includes organising rural poor into Self-help Groups (SHGs). It integrates various agencies - District Rural Development Agencies (DRDA), Banks, PRIs, non-government organizations (NGOs) and other semi-government organizations. This programme is basically a self-employment programme.

The objective of SGSY is to bring the existing poor families above the poverty line by providing them income generating assets through a mix of bank credit and government subsidy and to ensure that an assisted family has a monthly net income of at least Rs. 2,000. The families of Below Poverty Line (BPL) including artisans, identified through the BPL census are eligible for assistance under the scheme. While selecting the new activities priority may be given to those having inherent skill which is primarily constituted by the rural artisans. Subsidy under SGSY is uniform at 30 per cent of the project cost subject to a maximum of Rs. 7,500. In respect of SC and ST, it is 50 per cent subject to a maximum of Rs. 10,000. For groups, the subsidy is 50 per cent subject to a ceiling of Rs. 1.25 lakh. There is no monetary limit on subsidy for irrigation projects. SGSY is funded by the centre and states in the ratio of 75:25. Regarding the achievements of SGSY, it is observed that the total number of families assisted was 0.94 million in 2001-02 as compared to that of 1.66 million families assisted under IRDP in 1998-99.

The role of PRIs in the implementation of SGSY scheme are as under:

- The Gram Sabha will approve the list of BPL families.
- The list of key activities and the list of villages identified under the scheme in the Block should be approved by the Intermediate Panchayat.
- The list of *Swarozgaris* finally selected should be made available to the Gram Panchayat for placing it before the next Gram Sabha.
- The Gram Panchayat would actively monitor the performance of the *Swarozgaris* particularly repayment of loan.
- The District Panchayat will review the performance under this scheme in its General Body Meetings.

Analysis

The analysis of the data of SGSY in South Orissa are made under two heads:

(1) Physical and Financial Achievement under SGSY in South Orissa

The physical and financial achievement under SGSY in South Orissa during the year 2003-04 is given in Table 1.

Table 1 shows that during the year 2003-04, total investment under SGSY was Rs. 3,293.98 lakh in South Orissa. Out of this, the subsidy was Rs. 1,356.80 lakh and the credit was Rs. 1937.18 lakh. Of this, the highest investment was made in Ganjam district which was Rs. 1080.31 lakh and the lowest investment was made in Malkangiri district which was Rs. 195.16 lakh during the year 2003-04.

Table 1
Physical and Financial Achievement under SGSY in South Orissa during the year 2003-04

Sl. No.	*Districts*	*Investment (Rs. in Lakh)*		
		Subsidy	*Credit*	*Total*
1	Ganjam	444.15	636.16	1080.31
2	Gajapati	94.52	121.22	215.74
3	Koraput	248.32	283.39	531.71
4	Malkangiri	66.32	128.84	195.16
5	Nawarangpur	156.20	220.79	376.99
6	Rayagada	143.96	195.86	339.82
7	Boudh	71.95	131.73	203.68
8	Kandhamal	131.38	219.19	350.57
	Total	**1356.80**	**1937.18**	**3,293.98**

Source: *Economic Survey, 2004-05*, Directorate of Economics and Statistics, Orissa, Bhubaneswar, p. Anx.-34.

(2) Category-wise Progress and Achievement under SGSY in South Orissa

Category-wise progress and achievement under SGSY in South Orissa during the year 2003-04 is given in Table 2.

Table 2 reveals that during the year 2003-04, the total number of families covered under SGSY was 16,902 out of the targeted number of families was 14,487 in South Orissa. Of this, the coverage of SC families was 4,507, ST families was 6,944 and women families was 12, 575 in number under SGSY in South Orissa. During the year 2003-04, the highest coverage of families in the district of Ganjam which was 5,350 in number and the lowest coverage of families in the district of Boudh which was 823 in number under SGSY.

Conclusion

Several anti-poverty and wage employment programmes are being implemented in South Orissa under Panchayati Raj Department since 1980-81 to create income generating assets and employment on daily wage basis for identified beneficiaries of target groups so as to enable them to cross the poverty line. These anti-poverty programmes like IRDP, DWCRA, TRYSEM, SITRA, GKY and MWS have been merged into a single new scheme called SGSY with effect from 1-4-1999. During the year 2003-04, 16,902 number of *swarozgaries* have been assisted under SGSY scheme against the target of 14,487 number of *swarozgaries* in South Orissa. The total investment was Rs. 3293.98 lakh with subsidy and credit component of Rs. 1356.80 lakh and Rs. 1937.18 lakh respectively. Out of the above 16,902 number of *swarozgaries*, 4,507 number belongs to SC, 694 belongs to ST categories and 12,575 number belongs to women category in South Orissa.

Table 2

Category-wise Progress and Achievement under SGSY in South Orissa during the year 2003-04

(In numbers)

Sl. No.	*Districts*	*Target*	*Coverage of Families*			
			SC	*ST*	*Women*	*Total*
1	Ganjam	4.152	2221	330	4,895	5,350
2	Gajapati	1,434	184	905	916	1,469
3	Koraput	2,299	44	2,037	2,492	3,252
4	Malkangiri	907	350	373	445	880
5	Nawarangpur	2,04	299	1,418	1,952	2,115
6	Rayagada	1,510	49	992	1,426	1,597
7	Boudh	786	282	129	329	823
8	Kandhamal	1,395	278	760	220	1,416
	Total	**14,487**	**4,507**	**6,94**	**12,575**	**16,902**

Source: Economic Survey, 2004-05, Directorate of Economics and Statistics, Government of Orissa, Bhubaneswar, p. Anx-33

REFERENCES

Dhar, P.K., *Indian Economy and its Growing Dimensions*, Kalyani Publicatons, New Delhi, 2004.

Dhingara, I.C., *Indian Economy*, Sultan Chand & Sons, New Delhi, 2004.

Districts at a Glance, Government of Orissa, Bhubaneswar, 2005.

Economic Survey, Government of Orissa, Bhubaneswar, 2004-05.

Lekhi, R.K., *The Economics of Development and Planning*, Kalyani Publications, New Delhi, 2004.

Rudra, Dutta and Sundaram, K.P.M., *Indian Economy*, S. Chand & Sons, New Delhi, 2004.

Statistical Hand Book, 2004, Ganjam, Gajapati, Koraput, Malkangiri, Nawarangpur, Rayagada, Boudh and Kandhamal.

2

Rural Development Through Primary Education under Panchayati Raj System: A Case Study of Jayapur Panchayat

Balakrishna Padhi*

Panchayati Raj is a form of local government administered by a council or Panchayat elected in a democratic way. A Panchayat may cover one village or group of villages. It was introduced in 1959. Generally as a three-tier structure of local self-government at the village, block and district levels. These institutions are in existence in all-most-all states and union territories with vocations in structural pattern. The first tire at village level is commonly known as *Gram Panchayat*. The second tier is that at the block level in the form of *Panchayat Samitis* and the third tier as *Zilla Parishad* at the district level. Article 40 of the Indian Constitution directs the state "to take steps to organize Village Panchayats and endow them with such powers and authority as may be necessary to enable them to function as units of self-government." For almost four decades this Directive Principle of State Policy (DPSP) had to be implemented by state Governments in accordance with laws passes by state legislature in 1992. The Union Parliament brought about comprehensive amendments (73rd and 74th) in the Indian Constitution to introduce an uniform system of Local government. Apart from providing an institutional structure for these local units the Acts have also specified powers to be exercised by them. The Panchayati Raj is given the following

* UCG-NET Qualified and Research Fellow.

powers under the Eleventh Schedule for the rural society such as agriculture land improvement and implementation of land reforms, minor irrigation and water management, animal husbandry, dairying and poultry farming, fisheries, social forestry and farm forestry, small scale industries, *khadi* and cottage industries, rural housing, drinking water, fuel and fodder, roads and bridges, ferries and water ways, minor irrigation, rural electrification, non-conventional energy sources, poverty alleviation, primary education, vocational and adult education, technical education, libraries, cultural activities, market and fairs, health and sanitation, family welfare, women and child development, welfare of SC/ST and other weaker sections, public distribution system and maintenance of community assets. Similarly, the Twelfth Schedule enumerates various powers for urban panchayats.

Some specific features of the 73rd and 74th Amendments acts are: central funding for the panchayats, reservation of one-third seats for women, direct election conducted by State Election Commission, a final term of 5 years for all local bodies and greater autonomy in panchayat functioning.

Need of Panchayati Raj

Soon after India achieved its independence a vigorous search stared for an alternative model to the development of administration to cope with the growing needs of rural development on a gigantic scale in the country. The central administration cannot able to provide essential service towards rural society. Hence, the Panchayati Raj system plays crucial role for developing rural economy at grassroots level through various developmental works. On account of above reasons the Panchayati Raj Institution can be justified on several grounds like this:

(1) Firstly, we may note that modern government is expected to provide numerous services to the society. Some of these services require a kind of uniformity for the whole country and each would be provided the minimum of that service. Examples are of defence against foreign aggression, maintenance of law and order etc. Similarly, in rural area, there are other

services, which should allow for valuations, in local needs and aspirations. The State Government is wholly responsible for the socio-economic development of rural sector through Panchayati Raj system at grassroots level.

(2) Secondly, we should remember that Panchayati Raj provides the basic training ground for democracy people learn to appreciate their collective needs and responsibilities since we know that man is a social animal. They learn to see each others point of view they learn how to co-operate with each other for the realization of common good and community welfare. Thus, the existence of Panchayati Raj is essential in rural administration to make co-operation people in various development planning and polices.

(3) Thirdly, Panchayat is an institution, which is very economical; various plans and policies implemented by Panchayati Raj and policies implemented by Panchayati Raj and the participation of local people can be affected at much lower cost both in money and real terms. More over in itself Panchayati Raj is much less expensive system of local self-government than any other.

(4) Fourthly, Panchayati Raj can act as catalytic agent for transforming, the society's traditional values, an important reason for our economic backwardness lies in our superstitions, literacy, outmoded institutions etc. panchayats can act as great educative agencies in this respect programmes of literacy, adult education and so on.

The system of panchayati raj as not a new fangled thing, India has had the tradition of this system right through ages, during the British period, however, the system fell into discuss. The need for reviving the system of Panchayati Raj was being felt for quite some time, especially keeping in a view various advantages. The Mehta Committee, which went into the question of community development programme strongly, advocated the revival of Panchayati Raj system. The aim of community development programme is to bring about an integrated development of rural India it covers several aspects of rural life including economic and social ones and is aimed to bring about a qualitative change therein. Today, if we effectively utilize our decentralized system of governance through Panchayati Raj, we can take concentrated action for more effective delivery of basic services such as primary education, public health and healthcare providing safe drinking water and sanitation.

Rural Education under Panchayati Raj

Rural education in India has reached a threshold point. The spread of education in a vast country take ours has always been a challenging task. The successive central as well as the State Government have in the past followed the path of trial and error and have been able to identify special needs of the rural children in the field of education. The vast rural area, which is largely agrarian and shouldering the responsibility to provide employment to almost 60% of the national populations, is still, lagging behind in the spread of education.

The 86th Constitutional Amendment Act added Clause 21A to the right of life and guaranteed every child between the ages of 6-14 years, education up to the elementary stage as a fundamental right, the proposed amendment follow up central legislation on free and compulsory education. It is a constitutional commitment of our Government. Panchayati Raj has enabled the local self-government to take a more active part in the literacy movement, post literacy and continuing education programmes and also the schooling of the children. The government has initiated a number of programmes to achieve the goal of Universalization of Elementary Education (UEE) among which the Sarva Shiksha Abhijan (SSA) is the most recent one which effectively involving the Panchayati Raj Institution the School Management Committee, the Village Education Committee, the Parents Teachers Association. It is an attempt to provide and opportunity for improving human capabilities of the poorest children through provision of community owned quality education in a mission mode. It aims at achieving Universal Primary Education by 2007 and Universal Elementary Education by 2010, for successful implementation concerning Elementary Education effective monitoring coupled with efficient information system is essential. Several State Governments and Central Government have in past, initiated various efforts to meet the challenges of education particularly primary education in rural areas. However, the present governments seriousness to give the primary education a massive thrust is discernible in its imposing a 2% cess on all the central taxes to mop up at least 6000 crore rupees to be use in universalization of education. The funds will take care of the expansion and strengthening of Sarva Shiksha Abhiyan (SSA) and mid-day meal scheme.

Sarva Shiksha Abhiyan is one of the most important programmes of the Government despite SSA. There are other literacy programmes, adult and primary education programmes, i.e. amended by the government from time to time. The non-formal education (NFE) programme, pre-primary education including *Anganwadies* and *Balwadies* are implemented for development of rural education in Panchayat levels. A special programme District Primary Education Programme (DPEP) was launched in November 1994 with a view to overhauling the primary education system. The aim of the programme is achieving UEE through the district specific planning and target setting. The basic objectives of DPEP is:

(1) to provide primary education through either formal or non-formal stream to all children.

(2) To reduce difference in enrolment, dropout rated and learning achievements among gender and weaker section groups to less than five per cent.

(3) To reduce overall primary dropouts rate to less than 10%, it is the government finance 85% of the project cost as a grant to DPEP state implementation bodies. The rest of the cost is met by the State Government, the DPEP programme has been operational in backward districts with female literacy below the national average. One of the earliest such schemes known as Operation Black-board was started in 1987. It is aimed at improving certain minimum essential facilities in all primary schools. The scheme has brought about remarkable qualitative and quantitative improvement in primary education. In the remote and socio-

economically backward villages the *Shiksha Karmi* project aims at universalization and qualitative improvement of education to offset the problems of teacher absentees. The project used an alternative strategy by recruiting local youths known as *Shiksha karmis* in schools. They have been provided with training and supervisory support the mobilization and participation of the community in the functioning of primary schools is an important feature of this project.

Education in Jayapur Panchayat

Objectives of the Study

The principal objectives of the present study are:

(1) To examine improvement of primary education especially in rural areas under Panchayati Raj system.

(2) To study the enrolment and dropout rates of primary schools (Class V) especially SC/ST and socially backward classes under Panchayati Raj Institutions.

(3) To examine the glaring gender disparity of students in primary schools.

(4) To study the working of PRI in Jayapur Panchayat of Aska Block, to increase enrolment and attendance of the students and to hasten school dropouts.

Hypothesis

(1) That the interference of Panchayati Raj Institutions will enhance the enrolment of student in primary education.

(2) The Panchayati Raj Institution will able to check the enrolment/dropout ratio of SC/ST and general school going children.

Methodology

The present study covers all the primary schools if Jayapur Panchayat, which is in Aska Block of District Ganjam (Orissa). A case study has been conducted in Jayapur Panchayat, which contains four primary schools the data have been collected mainly from primary sources and have been collected from office file. Besides, this the data have been collected from teachers and students of the concerned schools through interview method, the simple statistical method as such as simple ratio, proportion and Lorenz Curve have been used to analyse the data, the data collected relate to enrolment and dropouts from 2000-01 to 2004-05.

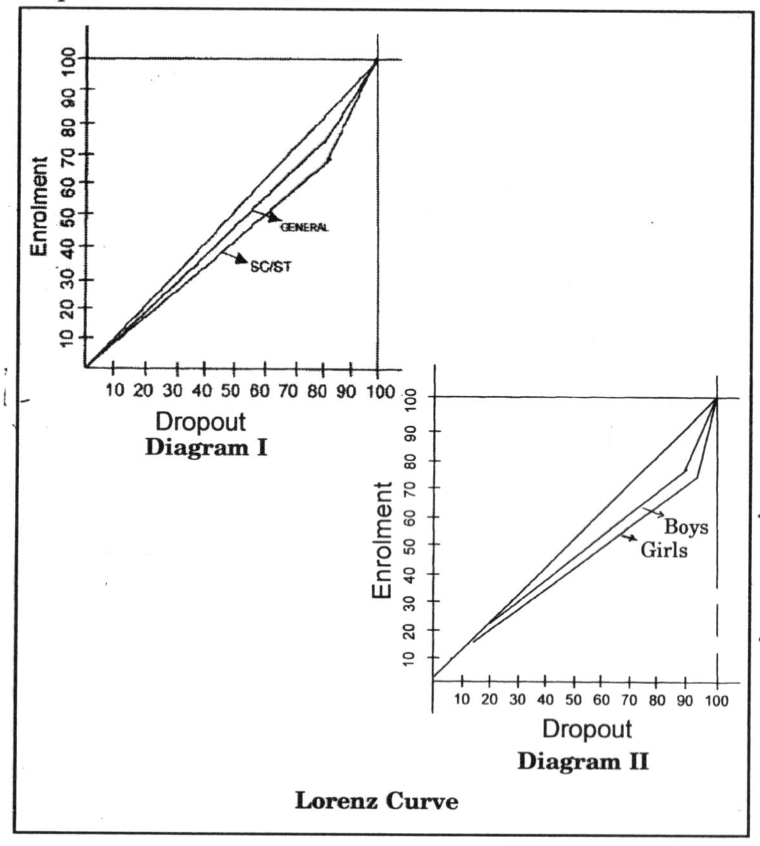

Lorenz Curve

Major Findings

The major causes and finding of the analysis are given in Table 1 below.

1. Table 1 reveals that there is a widening gap between enrolment and dropouts of school going children. Comparison has been made between the education of boys and girls among the dropouts. There are more girls then boys and most of the girl students comes from the vulnerable sections of the society. Over the period of 5 years. It is found from the study that the

proportion of dropout rates among girl students is higher in every year from 2000-01 to 2004-05.

Table 1
Gap between Enrolment and Dropouts of School Going Children (2000-2005)

	Primary (I-V) Enrolment			*Dropouts*		
Year	*Boys*	*Girls*	*Total*	*Boys*	*Girls*	*Total*
2000-01	574	270	844	132 (23)	138 (51.1)	270 (32)
2001-02	592	296	888	121 (26.5)	133 (45)	254 (28.6)
2002-03	606	314	920	118 (19.4)	127 (40.5)	245 (26.6)
2003-04	633	341	974	120 (19.4)	126 (37)	246 (25.3)
2004-05	658	363	1021	112 (17)	118 (32.6)	230 (22.5)

Source: Primary Data. (Office File).

Note: Figures within parentheses indicate percentages of dropouts.

2. Apart from this, mostly in the rural areas the girl children are found engaged in various house hold works like cooking, sweeping and cleaning, fetching water, wood collecting, taking cattle for grazing this is due to the fact that the girl students were deprived of the education, as their parents were thinking it is a wastage of time and money.

   The data reveal the there has been a fall in the dropout rate from 32 per cent in 2000-01 to 22.5 per cent in 2004-05 at the primary school level.

   Table 2 below reveals that the dropout rates at primary education in case of SC/ST students in 2000-01 is 66.5%. The dropout rates have been decreasing slowly to 50 per cent in 2004-05. The dropout rate of general students is very low in comparison to SC/ST students, which is 19.3 per cent in 2000-01 to 15.5 per cent in 2004-05.

3) The number of socio-cultural problems, which are greatly, influenced the disparity of education between boys and girls the path of parents or reluctant on the part of the parents to send their daughters to schools due to various social and cultural taboos is another reason of low enrolment of girl children.

Table 2
Dropout Rates at Primary Education in Case of SC/ST Students (2000-01 to 2004-05)

Year	*General*		*SC/ST*	
	Enrolment	*Dropout*	*Enrolment*	*Dropout*
2000-01	623	121 (19.3)	221	147 (66.5)
2001-02	625	117 (18.7)	263	151 (60)
2002-03	638	112 (17.7)	282	154 (54.8)
2003-04	667	112 (16.6)	307	158 (51.5)
2004-05	699	108 (15.5)	322	161 (50%)

Source: Primary data (Office File)

Note: Figures within parentheses indicate percentages of dropouts.

4) Generally rural areas are agricultural oriented. Most of the people are engaged in agricultural works, during the harvest season, the rural children instead of coming to schools engage themselves in agricultural works as well as home works and looking after younger siblings.

5) It is also found that in the rural areas, the people are poverty stricken and living below poverty line they are faced with some economic constraints, hence, the parents cannot able to send their girl child owing to heavy burden and low level of income.

6) Lack of literacy among rural people is another reason for decreasing enrolment of girl children, the illiterate people. However not willing to send their daughters to school, as they are bounded with age-old customs and traditions and their unwillingness to educate their daughters. Table 2 shows that comparison has been made between the general students and SC/ST students. The primary education of SC/ST students lags behind that of general students. The dropout rates of SSC/ST students have been higher than general students. The main reasons of low enrolment rate in case of SC/ST students are poverty, illiteracy and ignorance, age old traditions and customs, child labour etc. Apart from this migration of SC/ST students at

early age to sub-urban areas in search of works. Generally in brick industries and construction works and going abroad through labour contractors as bonded labourers, which is further handicaps the growth of primary education to a great extent in case of SC/ST and backward children.

Conclusion

In the light of the above findings, it is obvious that the condition of primary education under Panchayati Raj system has not changed significantly, universalization of primary education is still a distant goal in the country. More than fifty years of independence no substantial growth has been found in primary education, there are certain imbalances or disparities like, gender discrimination, economic disparities social inequalities and regional disparities which still continue to affect the educational system in our country. Education is one of the catalyst factors for human resource development, which comprises better health nutrition, good environment, and improved socio-economic opportunities for all. Particularly after independence literacy has been viewed as the essential component of the overall architecture of development planning in India. The government has recognized the role of woman and women education in the process of rural development. The problem of education of girl children in primary level has also been exacerbated due to low enrolment and high dropouts rates, the same thing has been seen in case of SC/ST and socially and economically backward school going children. Even after the implementation of universalization of elementary education. No significant achievement has been attained. So far, in the present context, the government should promote rural education at primary level through free and compulsory education and special attention should be given to improve women education to avoid glaring gender disparity in rural area. Since literacy is the most important and effective measure to bring out economic progress of a country. This is need of the hour the government should have to take crucial steps to boost up primary education.

3

Panchayati Raj Institutions in Orissa: Issues and Challenges

Dr. Dasarathi Bhuyan*

The success of a democratic system legally depends upon the existence and efficient operation of a system of local government at the grassroot levels. Local self-government is a system of direct and active involvement of the people of a local area into the administration of local affairs, for the satisfaction of local needs with the help of local resources and through organised local efforts. Through their participation in the administration of local government, the people get psychologically and socially involved in the process of politics and their achievements at the local level always contribute towards the achievement of the goal of nation building.

The makers of our Constitution were fully aware of the imperative necessity of organising a system of local self-government at the grassroot level and using it as a solid foundation for ensuring the stability, strength and health of the Indian liberal democratic political system. The Constitution of India gives a directive to the state to establish, maintain and operationalise a system of local government, and the Indian state has been maintaining a system of local government in both urban and rural areas. Rural local government in India is known by the popular name Panchayati Raj. The Panchayati Raj Institutions in India are the prime instruments of decentralisation at the grassroot level. The launching of community development programme on 2nd October, 1952 get the stage for the organisation of Panchayati Raj. In 1952,

* Lecturer in Political Science, Belaguntha Science College, Belaguntha, Ganjam, Orissa.

during the First Five-year Plan, the programme of community development was started. It aimed to create among the rural people an active interest in various national schemes of economic planning and social reconstruction. But people were not active and willing participants in plan implementation at the village level. A committee was appointed in January 1957 to review the working of the community development programme under the headship of Sri Balwant Rai Mehta. This team suggested the establishment of Panchayati Raj with adequate delegation of powers. It also recommended the setting up of elected and organically linked democratic bodies at the village, block and the district levels. The recommendations of the committee were accepted and the Panchayati Raj system was first implemented in Rajasthan in 1959. In Orissa, it was implemented on 26th January 1961. There are three main organs in the framework of Panchayati Raj - *Gram Panchayat, Panchayat Samiti* and *Zilla Parishad.*

The 73rd Constitutional Amendment Act is the most significant event in the history of democratic decentralisation. It gave constitutional status to the Panchayati Raj Institutions. The following are the main features of the 73rd Amendment Act of 1993:

1. The Gram Sabha will be a body comprising of all the adult members registered as voters of panchayats.
2. There shall be three-tier system of panchayats at three levels, i.e. village, intermediate and district levels.
3. Seats in panchayats at all the three levels shall be filled by direct election.
4. In all the panchayats seats would be reserved for women.
5. Every panchayat shall have a uniform five-year term and in the event of dissolution, elections will be compulsory held within six months.
6. Independent Election Commission will be established in the state for superintendence, direct and control of elections and preparation of the three electoral rolls.
7. Specific responsibilities will be entrusted to the panchayats to prepare plans for economic development

and social justice in respect of matters listed in the Eleventh Schedule. After the 10th Schedule to the constitution the 11th Schedule is added, which enjoy rural bodies to perform 29 functions.

8. In each state, a Finance Commission will be established with in one year from the passage of this act and then after every five years to determine the principles on the basis of which adequate financial resources would be ensured for the Panchayats.

Issues and Challenges

The working of Panchayati Raj institutions are not satisfactory. There is slow progress of Panchayati Raj Institutions in Orissa. Its success is yet to be seen. Unfortunately, for more reasons than one, the Panchayati Raj has not been able to fulfil the expectations aroused by the planners. The main issues and challenges responsible for the failure of this experiment can be analysed as under:

1. **Illiteracy and ignorance**: the widespread illiteracy and ignorance among the rural people remained a major hindrance in the way of the successful operation of Panchayati Raj. It prevented the people from becoming an active and willing partners in this system.
2. **Excess of governmental control**: It is another hurdle in its successful working of Panchayats, the government often interferes arbitrarily in their daily working. This control kills the initiative of the local bodies, independent minded public spirited persons are not prepared to be members of these local bodies.
3. **Lack of funds**: The shortage of funds is another serious defect of Panchayati Raj. Their meager financial resources render them incapable of undertaking developmental activities, as their income is so small, they cannot provide all amenities of life to citizens and consequently no enthusiasm is created among the people.
4. **Inexperienced representatives**: The inability of the representatives elected by the rural people to comprehend fully the programmes and policies of the

Panchayati Raj and their apathy towards their duties as representatives of the people together made the working of the Panchayati Raj Institutions inefficient.

5. **Lack of political awareness**: Rural poverty, illiteracy and ignorance were together responsible for a low level of political awareness among the people of rural areas, this prevented the adoption of Panchayati Raj by them as a system of self-government and self-development.

6. **Party politics**: Panchayati Raj Institutions are often battle grounds of political parties. This party-rivalrydivides the villages into various functions and groups, and saps the vitality of co-operative village life, this often result in favouritism, nepotism and parochialism.

7. **Corruption**: The people in our country have low moral standards and as such, there is a lot of corruption in public life. People manage to get various contracts from local bodies, bringing all those whose are concerned with the giving of such contracts.

8. **Small size of the block areas**: In the structure of Panchayati Raj, the responsibility to implement development plans and programmes was largely vested with the Panchayat Samiti, which worked at the block or taluk or tehsil level. Each block was a small area and its Panchayat Samiti, often found the task of formulating development plans for such a small area difficult and problematic.

9. **Benefits mostly to one class**: The objective of securing the involvement of all the people of rural areas in the process of securing development through community efforts was put into practice but it benefited only the rich landlords and the upper classes of the rural people. The rich landlords dominated the elections to the panchayats and thereby became the dominant actors in the working of the other two institutions of the Panchayati Raj. The poor people failed to really get involved in it.

10. **Caste-ridden**: A serious problem of Panchayati Raj is that it is caste-ridden today. High caste men do not

allow the low caste people the privileges they enjoy. During the panchayat elections, caste often plays prominent role.

11. **Structural defects**:
    (1) Ineffectiveness of the Gram Sabha.
    (2) Nominated character of the Panchayat Samitis and Zilla Parishad.
    (3) Lack of adequate powers particularly for the Panchayat Samitis.
    (4) Lack of trained and efficient staff.
    (5) Economic dependence upon the government.
    (6) Irregular elections.
    (7) Frequent and prolonged suspension of the Panchayati Raj Institutions.
    (8) Lack of good relationship between the Panchayati Raj staff and the rural people.
    (9) Working of Panchayati Raj Institutions more as governmental agencies and less as popular and public institutions.

Problem of Women Representation

Reservation of one-third seats in panchayat for them is a salient revolution to improve their status. But scholars have raised the issue of women's representation in Panchayati Raj Institutions and viewed that the objectives of reservation for women are not truly fulfilled, women share responsibilities of village administration in addition to their farm and domestic responsibilities. They attend to peoples problem and there is no fixed hour of work. It disturbs the harmony of home and family life. Also they feel physically insecure when they go out to attend panchayat meetings.

In reality women representatives are ornamental in nature and political consciousness is found lacking among them. They are affected by the caste and class divisions feudal attitudes, patriarchal nature of the family and village social environment, ethnic and religious separatism and the like, they are members on record only. Allegedly, they are not consulted while taking decision. Thus, women representatives are not free from male dominance in the Panchayat institutions and no significant change in the power equation is observed in the villages. It is felt need to make women aware of their role in all spheres of panchayat activities.

Suggestions for the Removal of these Problems

It is widely felt that party politics is an important factor contributing to the downfall of Panchayati Raj system. The election fought on party lines in Panchayats divides the people in the villages. The election held on party basis help build up parties and not people. In the process one finds the rampant misuse of muscle power, money power, casteism and communalism in the panchayat elections. This is why P.R. system without party politics needs to be encourages. Since, in reality Panchayati Raj system cannot be declined from the party politics, it is the moral responsibility of every person to try that honest and morality upright people must remain in Panchayati Raj. Appropriate training programmes for all functionaries at the Panchayat level should be organised regularly.

The government should also change its former attitudes towards the PRIs. It should give up its attitude of hostility or indifference. The officials concerned including the District Collector should be directed to help the local bodies in every possible way. Excessive government control and interference of the Government in the day to day administration of local bodies are also sometime responsible for failure of local bodies.

The PRIs need better personnel as well as a better office organisation and methods. Certain qualifications should be laid down for recruitment to the staff of the Panchayati Raj Institutions. Special provisions should be made for the training of personnel of Panchayati Raj institutions. The Panchayati Raj institutions should have adequate finance at their disposal to take up manifold developmental activities. They should be allowed to collect more taxes and make their budgets self-sufficient. In case of deficit, the government should readily come forward to help without hesitation.

There cannot be any dramatic movement in the system just by including women members in Gram Panchayat institutions. At the same time, it is also essential to shed certain stereotyped prevailing nations about role and importance of women in socio-economic development. Women should be encourages to play a more active part. The male representatives have to establish a support with the female representatives and give due respect and attention to their views. Of course there is some awareness among women due to reservation for them in PRIs. But there is need for appropriate training and education relating to different aspects of functioning of panchayats to make women members conscious enough of their effective role and representation in the Panchayat Samiti. This kind of training can be organised at the district or block level immediately following the election, we have to understand that women representatives can play a vital role in the formulation and implementation of various women and child development programmes. This would increase the efficacy of such programmes. For instance, the women representatives and Gram Panchayats should have sufficient control over the primary education, primary health care and running of the public distribution system. The Eleventh Schedule contains 29 items including the above-mentioned items. But the transfer of these subjects has not been made legally finding.

In rural areas, people in general are unaware of the kinds of developmental activities undertaken at panchayat level. The general notion prevalent among them is that the *Sarpanch* and Secretary are always money-oriented. In order to remove this suspicion, the functionaries of Gram Panchayat should maintain transparency and make villagers aware of the developmental works being undertaken at the panchayat level. For this, awareness camps should be organised. Loans under various anti-poverty programmes should be sanctioned on the basis of recommendations of the Gram Panchayat. The right of evaluation, viability-appraisal and sanction of developmental work at the level of Gram Panchayat should be vested in them. The panchayat should have also sufficient control and supervision over the governmental servants such as VLW, VAW, ANM, LSI, ICDS, Junior Engineer, Fishery Development Officer, Agriculture Extension Officer and the like working at GP level. The main objectives of panchayat to involve people and to cultivate in them initiative and self-reliance should not be relegated into the background. This will help expedite and ensure smooth running of various developmental activities in the village.

It is felt that judicial and legal powers should be given to Gram Panchayat. But the Gram Panchayat should not succumb to pressure from any quarter and deal with disputes faithfully, truthfully and honestly, because in the past experience shows discrimination in awarding punishment of weaker sections.

Mobilisation and proper utilisation of financial resources is the major problem of Gram Panchayat, where resources are limited in quantum because of poor taxation and poor realisation of tax. PRIs depend largely on government grants. The objective of Gram Panchayat can be realised if more financial powers are given to Gram Panchayat. Panchayat bodies must be very clear about their own needs, their existing resources, additional resources they can tap with and without states assistance, grants as also their own investment programmes.

Panchayati Raj system necessarily aims at decentralised planning and participation of people in the planning process. So, panchayat has to play a major role in plan formulation and its approval at the district and block level planning. Also, it has to play important role at the implementation stage. Significantly, developmental works have to be executed through the local people. The financial accounts, i.e. sources of receipts and uses of funds should be made available for information to local peoples who have a meaningful say in the decision-making regarding allocation of funds. This would go some way in making the role of women more effective.

The panchayat body has to find out all possible means to create its own assets to generate additional income through various investments. The financing of such products can be sought from the financial institutions. The right to raise financial resources through tax and non-tax means as per the existing PP Act should also come into full force. Non-agricultural goods produce in the villages such as bricks, traditional brass utensils, pottery items, handloom, handicrafts, coir/jute ropes and the like may be brought within the ambit of Gram

Panchayat taxation. Different types of raw materials produced in the village and used in the urban industrial centers generate a tax revenue for the state government. Some portion of this revenue may be diverted to the Gram Panchayats. Besides, certain income generating assets namely village orchards, village ponds, bazars, ghats and the like are under the control of the Revenue Department. For additional income generation, these assets may be transferred for management to the Gram Panchayats or given out on lease. Taxes like motor vehicle taxes, sales tax, excise revenue should also be shared with panchayats.

Indian political system has within it a well-organised and well-functioning systems of rural local government. These grass-root level institutions serve as instruments for providing political education and training to the people of Orissa as well as these acts as very useful means for securing the socio-economic development of Orissan villages. No doubt their working has not been fully successful in securing the desired goals, nevertheless, they have the potential to develop and become stronger and efficient organs of local development with local resources, local efforts and through local representatives. The 73rd Constitutional Amendment Act has made a bold attempt to ensure their continuity, stability, representativeness and autonomy with a view to enable them function as valuable systems of self-governance, by giving people chances to manage their own affairs. Panchayati Raj Institution strengthens their sense of freedom and makes them vigilant of their liberty in the national sphere as well. Judge learned Hand rightly says, "Liberty lies in the hearts of men and women, when it dies there, no constitution, no law, no court can save it and no constitution, no law, and no court can even do much to help it."

REFERENCES

Barik, Sarmistha and Chitrasen Pasayat, "Empowerment of common people", *Orissa Review*, BBSR, Feb-1987, pp. 2-3.

Dandekar, V.M., "Unitary elements in a federal constitution", *Economy and Political Weekly*, Oct. 31, 1987.

Gangrade, K.D., "Power to the powerless down of Participatory democracy", *Kurukhshetra*, New Delhi, Vol. 43(7) 1995, pp. 3, 7.

Ghai, K.K., *Democracy, Nation Building and Ideologies*, Kalyani Publishers, Ludhiana, pp. 86, 109.

Maheswar, S.R., *Rural Development in India*, p. 53.

Mehta, U., "The impact of the Panchayatii Raj on Rural India", In: A.R. Desai (ed), *Rural sociology in India*, Popular Prakashan, Bombay, 1984.

Mishra, Aditya Keshari, "Working of Gram Panchayats in Orissa", *Orissa Review*, BBSR, p. 93.

Mishra, R., "Devolution of power to women in Panchayati Raj in Orissa: challenges and opportunities", *Kurukhsetra*, New Delhi, Vol 47(B), 1998, pp. 19-24.

Rout, B.C., *New Rudiments of Politics*, Nalanda, Cuttack, pp. 85, 102.

4

Panchayati Raj Institutions: Issues and Challenges

Subhrabala Behera*

Panchayati Raj Institutions (PRIs) in India refer to a statutory, multi-tier administrative structure entrusted with developmental duties and responsibilities by the state legislatures. It is the management at local affairs by the representatives of the rural areas elected by the rural people themselves. The Panchayati Raj system has considerably helped in strengthening Indian democracy at the grassroot level. Panchayats have been the backbone of the Indian villages. The 73rd constitutional amendment is certainly a landmark in devolution of powers to entrust the responsibility to the Gram Panchayat at the bottom, block or Panchayat Samiti at the intermediary and Zilla Parishad at the top level in the three-tier Panchayati Raj Institution for planning, development, monitoring and supervision by focusing on the improvement of the conditions at the rural areas and thereby bringing about a sea change in the quality of life of the people. After this amendment, panchayats have become important instruments for social change and development. Article 243(Z) suggests that panchayats should gradually become institutions of self-government. According to the amendment and conformity acts by states, administrative and financial powers to be developed to panchayats.

Evolution of PRI in India

India has a rich legacy of local self-government, the vastness of the modern state and the growing complexities

*Lecturer in Political Science, KPAN College, Bonkai, Khurda, Orissa.

with its manifold activities has made it impossible for a single governmental organisation to deal efficiently with all its problems. This arise the necessity of creating smaller units of administration. The role of local administration in Indian situation has special importance as India is considered to be the largest democratic country in the world. Its task is very difficult as India lives in villages having by basic amenities.

Panchayati Raj system existed in India even in ancient times. Panchayat has been an oldest administrative unit of the village. The local authorities is ancient and medieaval India were corporate authorities and were based on manhood suffrage. Periodization of village administration can be made into four phases, namely: (a) Ancient period, (b) Muslim period, (c) British period and (d) post-Independence period.

(a) **Ancient period**: The existence to rural settlement may be traced back, not lonely to vedic times but also to the pre-historic moments of Beluchistan and Lower Sind. Through Veda and *Mahabharata*, we can get an outline of the systems of village and inter-village organisation. Manu in his book *Manu Samhita* distinguishes between three kinds of settlement - village (*grama*), town (*pura*) and city (*nagara*). Kautilya also in his *Arthashasthra* narrated the functions of village institutions.

(b) **Muslim period**: Muslim rule in India lasted for more than five centuries. A significant change that Muslim rule brought about was in the relationship between the villagers on the one hand and the urban centres and the ruling classes on the other hand.

(c) **British period**: *Zamindari* and *Ryotwari* systems were introduced by the Britishers which gave to a new feudal economic order in the rural society. The age-old rural administration received in a revised form, power again began to be decentralized to local self-governing bodies to look after primary education, public health, etc. The starting point of local self-government was the establishment of District Local Fund Committee under Bombay Act III of 1889. The Lord Rippon's Resolution of 18th May, 1882 also clearly enunciated the principle of self-government.

(d) **Post-Independence period**: India had born (during the freedom) the concept of a new political theory "Villages on". A new experiment was takes up by the Father of the Nation Mahatma Gandhi who knew every Indian village minorately well and could feel about the world. The stream of village government and administration was realised through Article 40 of the Indian Constitution in the chapter on the Directive Principle of State Policy (Chapter IV) in post-Independence period which empowered the State Government to organise panchayats and endow them with such powers and authority as may be necessary to enable them to function as units of local government. A number of laws were passed in the Parliament to implement this provisions of the Constitution. The introduction of democratic decentralisation in its present shape owes its origin to the report of Mehta Study Team. In January 1957, Balwant Rai Mehta Committee was appointed to examine the working of community development and Nation Extension Service. On 2nd October, 1959, it recommended a three-tier structure of Panchayati Raj Institutions, there is no uniform pattern of Panchayati Raj in India. Panchayati Raj system first adopted in Rajasthan.

It is evident from the following facts:

(1) it has created awareness regarding the working of democratic institutions at the grass-root level.

(2) It has created opportunities for participation and gain experiences as representatives at the grass-root level

(3) Panchayati Raj has helped in the development of the spirit of self-confidence among the people.

(4) Panchayati Raj is the best means of giving training in administration to the people. It provides an opportunity to the people for making and executing development plans of deciding cases and screening the day-to-day administration of the local affairs.

(5) Panchayati Raj system is the real foundation of Indian democracy and on its successful performance depends on the working of Indian democratic system.

Aims and Objectives of PRI

(1) Panchayati Raj stimulates self-education this is to develop the political consciousness of the masses. It also inculcates self-reliance, integrity and courage among the people.

(2) It has shifted the centre of gravity to the villages i.e. democratic decentralization.

(3) The Panchayati Raj aims at eradicating excessive paper work, delay, red tappism, aloofness by vesting administrative power in popular representation.

(4) It ensures popular participation and encourages local leadership.

(5) Unless villages develop and prosper, the country will not be progressive. In short, it aims at an overall development and reconstruction of villages.

Functions

Different states have different approaches and developed powers and functions according to their requirements. As it is, the Acts on Panchayati Raj contain certain detailed list of functions assigned to respective tires. They generally comprise functions as: (1) obligatory or compulsory functions, and (2) optional functions.

The functions include effective coordination of programmes at the local level between related sectors such as sanitation, safe drinking water, women and child development, promote education, health care, road and bridge etc. There are also enabling provisions to the effect that the government could entrust additional functions and responsibilities under any law or laws for the time being and issue necessary orders and directions.

Panchayati Raj in Orissa

The Orissa Panchayat Samiti and Zilla Parishad Act was passed in 1959 which received the assent of the Governor on the 15th Feb., 1960. This act came into force and Orissa worked out this scheme of the 26th Jan., 1961. In Orissa Panchayati Raj has three tier systems: Gram Panchayat, Panchayat Samiti and Zilla Parishad or District Advisory Council, this can be illustrate in the following chart:

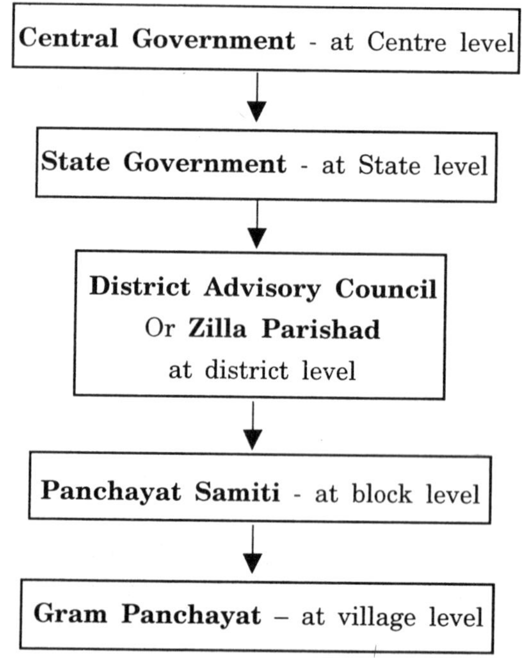

The Zilla Parishad

The Zilla Parishad was that the apex of the Panchayati Raj system in Orissa. But the 1968 Amendment abolished the Zilla Parishads and substituted in its place the District Advisory Council for each district. The Zilla Parishad consists the members, collector of the district, MLAs and MPs under that district, all Chairmen of the Panchayat Samities within the district, all Chairmen of Municipal Councils, the presidents of the Central Co-operative Banks, the presidents of the District Land Mortgage Banks, 1/3rd non-official seats are reserved for women. Zilla Parishad performs different types of functions like, to advise government regarding developmental and other activities referred to it, to consider and advise government to execute development activities effectively, to appoint smaller committees among themselves for specific matter. The meeting shall be three times in a year which convened by the Collector. He has a well quit hierarchy in the district which may be illustrated in the following chart:

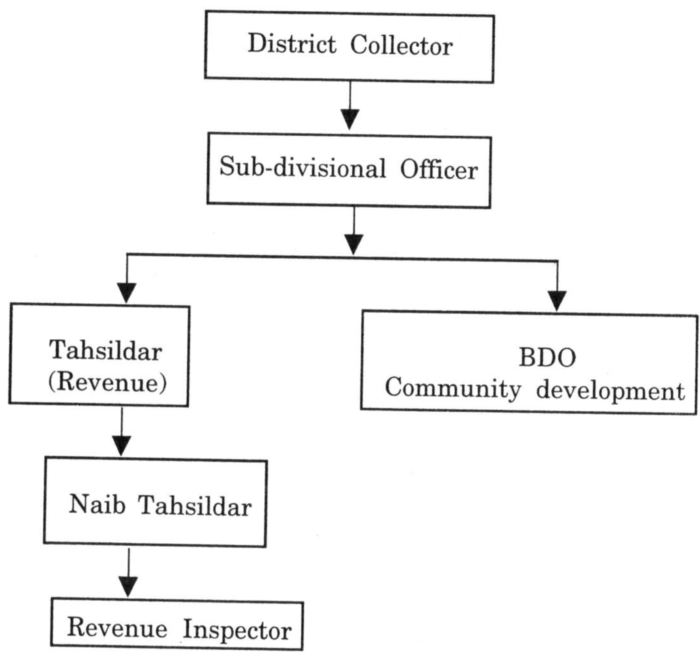

Gram Panchayat

Gram Panchayats are at the bottom of the three-tier organisation at Panchayati Raj. There must be 11 to 25 words in a panchayat and their tenure is five years. Officers of the panchayats are: *Sarpanch*, *Naib Sarpanch*, ward members who are directly elected by the people, the Gram Panchayat shall hold meetings in every month by preside of *Sarpanch* it performs two types of functions. Optional and obligatory like, (1) construction, cleaning and lighting of public streets, (2) provision for medical relief, sanitation and prevention of diseases, (3) registration of births and deaths, (4) promotion of cooperative farmings, (5) planting trees by the sides of the roads etc. The structure of Gram Panchayat can be show in the following chart:

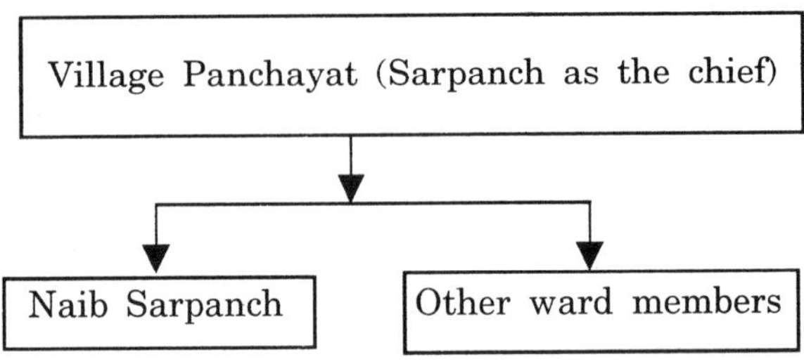

Gram Panchayat collects revenues through different sources, these are: (1) collection or taxes in the village areas, (2) by imposing licence fees, (3) from village markets, *ghats*, ponds or distdung and (4) granting aid from government.

The Challenges

While decentralized institutions may be more susceptible to local participation and control by the same token they may be captive to the local structure of power says Arkadie. The drawbacks of centralized power (insensitively to local needs and ignorance of local capacities) have their counterparts in the skewed access that can arise from local systems of power prejudice. With more power and resources and less accountability.

Panchayat Samiti

The government decides each district into smaller number of local areas known as a block. Every block shall have a Panchayat Samiti consisting of the members, BDO, employees of different departments. *Sarpanch* of the Gram Panchayats, chairmen of the municipalities situated in that block, chairmen of each of the NAC, 1/3rd seats of non-official members are reserved for women. Chairman is the head of Panchayat Samiti shall be elected directly by the people. Samiti does different types of functions like (1) planning, execution and supervision of development programmes, schemes and works (1) management, control and spread of primary education in the block, (2) supervise of Gram Panchayats and their budgets, (3) to manage trusts and endowments and (5) to vaccinate and register births and deaths. The composition at Panchayat Samiti may be given in the following chart:

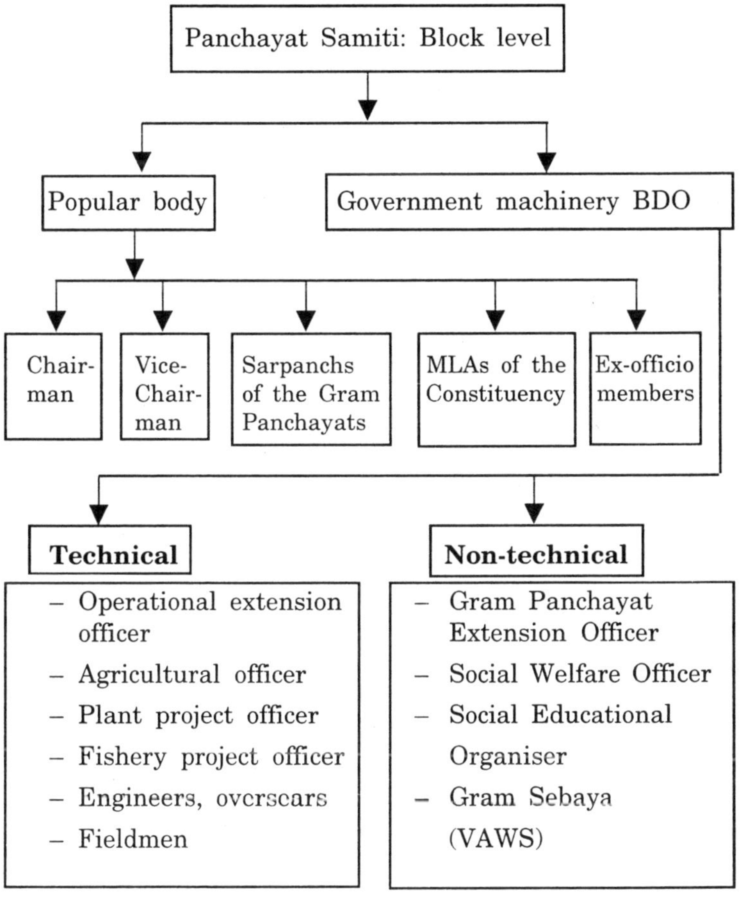

The Panchayati Raj institution may become a bed of harassment of the SCs, STs and women who have no protection. According to Pravin Sheth, funnelling or resources and powers from the centre on a vast scale to the panchayats which are not prepared and experienced to use them in proper and competent ways will create massive problems of misuse, wastage and financial mismanagement. In a way, corruption along with power will be decentralized if institutional degeneration is not reversed and supportive institutions not promoted.

Framework for Action

Democracy, service motive, member education and participation, empowerment (especially of the poor), etc. continue the framework for an action plan for institution building at the grass roots level. It is noteworthy that co-operators and promotional agencies like the co-operative initiative panel are campaigning for comprehensive reform of the system on the light of liberalization; however political will is laying in the adoption of model co-operative laws envisaging greater autonomy and business orientation in their operations. Though the role of training has been fully recognized in the scheme of Panchayati Raj, the outflow of trainees from centres like the National Institute of Rural Development is very disappointing, political and cultural outfits who have a dubious post of caste/fraction ridden also need reform. The state-PRI relations require appropriate redefinition in the new context.

Problems

There is slow progress of local self-government not only in Orissa but also in India. The following are certain serious defects for which arises problems:

(1) People in India are illiterate, conservative and lack civic consciousness. So at the time of elections they vote according to their families, castes and personal relatives.

(2) Excess of governmental control over local governments is another hurdles in its successful working.

(3) The shortage of funds is another serious defect. For their meager finance they cannot provide all amenities of life to citizens and consequently no enthusiasm is created among the people.

(4) Local self-institutions are often bottle ground of political parties. The result in favourism, nepotism and parochialism.

(5) A serious criticism of the Panchayati Raj is caste ridden today. High casteness does not allow the law caste people the privileges they enjoy.

(6) Lastly, the employees of local bodies are untrained and inefficient.

Suggestions for Removal of these Defects

(1) A minimum standard of education is necessary which will kill illiteracy, backwardness and conservatism of the people.

(2) The control of government over local bodies should be minimised.

(3) The local bodies need better personnel as well as a better organisation and methods.

(4) Local bodies should have adequate finance at their disposal to take up manifold developmental activities.

(5) People should be free from corruption and be honest, moralism, truth binding, vigilant and well-informed.

Conclusion

The PRI may have weakness still it will be a vital force in shaping and developing the richer and prosperous life of Indian people. It acts like the grassroot of democracy and a time may come when J.P. Narayan is dream of "Grama Sabha to Lok Sabha" will materialise through it.

5

An Alley on Panchayati Raj

Subhasmita Mahapatra*

We need one and uniqueness. That may be in big resources or in small in politics, viz. a small name but large local political contribution is Panchayati Raj. It is the incrustation in ruling.

Historically, Panchayati Raj system has been in existence in rural India from ancient times. The village was considered the basic unit of self-government, the *Arthashastra* also outlines the functions and duties of local self-governing institutions. The Village Panchayat enjoyed a lot of autonomy. Most of the religious, cultural and economic activities were handled with care and efficiently by them. The Central Government whose chief leader was the king himself, was dependent on information furnished by local villages and city boards. The system was considered ideal by the Moghuls too. Therefore, they instructed the central and provincial authorities to keep their hands off the local village functionaries. The British Government did not disturb the three-tier system. The leaders of Indian national movement were aware of the system. Hence they committed themselves to establish a system of democracy where people at the grassroot level could be involved in the development process.

Jawaharlal Nehru was one of the chief architects of Panchayati Raj in India. He hailed it as 'the most historical and revolutionary step in the content of new India'. Nehru held the view that more democracy would not make much headway unless the people's institutions at the grassroots could raise resources locally as was done in the past. The villages

* Student, K.S.V.B, College, Bhanjanagar, Ganjam, Orissa.

formed basic units each one able to derive enough direct benefit for local agriculture and crafts to be self-sufficient. He felt that villages should not be dependent on grants from States and Centre.

After independence, an effort was made to recognize and revitalise the Panchayati Raj system. In fact, Panchayati Raj became a prerequisite for execution of the Community Development Programmes (CDP) started in 1952. The CDP was followed by National Extension Service (NES) to build up an administrative system to tackle the problem of growth and development at the local level. A committee was appointed in 1957 under Balwant Rai Mehta to go into the working of the Community Development Projects and National Extension Service with a view to ensure economy and efficiency. The committee recommended a three-tier system of rural local government namely Village Panchayat at village level, the Panchayat Samiti at block level and the Zilla Parishad at the district level. Following the teams report and because of Nehru's interest in CDP all State governments except Meghalaya, Mizoram and Nagaland quickly passed Panchayati Raj legislation one after another.

Elected directly by and from the villagers, the Panchayats are responsible for promotion of agriculture, rural industries, provision of medical relief, maternity, women and child welfare, maintaining common grazing grounds, village roads, tanks, wells and provision for sanitation. In some places they also provide primary education and collect land revenue. Now the Panchayati Raj Institutions (PRIs) are also involved in antipoverty programmes for IRDP and the rural development programmes. There are at present 2.20 lakh Village Panchayats, 5,500 Panchayat Samities and 375 Zilla Parishads. The Panchayati Raj Institutions have been given statutory authority in many states for raising finance through taxation, levy of cess etc. on houses, lands, village markets, faire festivals and on sale of goods.

However, after a brief period of euphoria and glitter, the Panchayati Raj Institutions (PRIs) passed into oblivion, in 1977, another committee was appointed under Ashok Mehta during the Janata Dal regime to review the working of PRIs and suggest measures for improvement after identifying the shortenings. The committee reported some important causes for the decline of the PRIs. It stated that the activities of the PRIs were meagre, their resources poor and overall attention given to them almost nil. For eradicating corruption, inflating costs, delays, internal functions, rivalaries PRIs, is a threatening towards MLAs and MPs. Thus they started exercising their influence to destroy the PRIs.

Inspite of this negative role of the states, a powerful opinion existed in the country that democracy and development cannot be strengthened without Panchayati Raj.

Late Prime Minister Rajiv Gandhi felt a need to revitalise the PRIs. The Indian Constitution passed 73rd and 74th Amendment Acts in 1992. These acts gave constitutional status to Panchayati Raj Institutions. Success of Panchayati Raj depends on (a) regular election, (b) generation of public opinion, (c) local bodies becoming responsive and (d) adequate funds.

The critics point out that rural India has a power structure of landlords, moneylenders and anti-social elements. These anti-social forces will try to conquer Panchayati Raj Institutions, rig the elections and terrorise the voters. Rural India has a social reality of tyranny and oppression. It has to be borne in mind that new power and funds will make local powerful people more tyrannical. However, it remains to be seen whether the voters will learn to exercise their rights properly.

In spite of all this, no one has so far said that Panchayati Raj is not required, everyone feels the importance of PRIs for grassroot development, PRIs can certainly become an instrument of social change in rural India. The key to the success of this enterprise is a national consensus. People should rise above prejudices and doubts and devote themselves to the task of marking Panchayati Raj a success. Development in India can certainly receive a new impetus 'through democratic decentralisation'. Hence, in all respect it is the best alley of Democracy.

REFERENCE

Dhilon, R.S., *An Alley and Ambition on Panchayati Raj,* DGP Publications.

6

Panchayati Raj Institution and Tribal Development

Pradeep Patnaik* and G.C. Panda**

The economic problems of the tribes are multi-factorial and multi-dimensional in nature. They have lost their socio-economic and cultural grounds, in the race of the economic modernization and social advancements. Inadequacy of the amenities of the life such as sanitation, education, health, transport, drinking water and hygiene, environment in the tribal regions cause undesirable loss of human lives in the form of the low life expectancy, high infant mortality, pre-natal and post-natal deaths. Lack of generation of employment opportunities and disproportionate distribution of income and output keep the tribes in the loosing end of the development. Deficiency of integrative approaches in the field of social sectors (education and health) cause wastage of resources both human and natural to a greater extent in tribal regions.

As PRIs by their active role in understanding the problems of the masses and articulation of their responses can ensure development for tribal people with a human face. PRIs help to create awareness about the rights and opportunities, legal means of enforcement, monitoring and re-designing of policies at ground level because of its profound impact on socio-economic life of people. Properly implemented, it can pave the ways for social sector development women empowerment and reduce gender discrimination in other sectors of life PRIs are the

* Lecturer of Economics, K.D. Science College, Pachilima, Ganjam, Orissa.

**Lecturer of Economics, AMCS College, Tikabali, Kandhamal, Orissa.

micro-institution meant to fight against poverty injustice, inequality and economic disparity by narrowing down the intra- and inter-community economic gap. To conclude, PRIs have created an opportunity, especially for downtrodden to take their own policy decisions by carrying their economic visions forward.

Profile of the District and the Block under Study

Indian is the land of tribes. They are concentrated mainly the central belt of India and constituting nearly 8 per cent to our population as per 2001 Census. The State of Orissa is the second largest home for the tribes, the percentage is 22.23 next to Madhya Pradesh. So they cannot be kept them isolated if we intend to develop Orissan economy.

The district of Boudh Kandhamal was first formed on 1st January, 1948. Later on this district was called Phulabani district. After 1st April, 1994 with creation of Boudh district, this popularly known Phulabani district has been rechristened as the Kandhamal district, aptly so because this mountain terrain is mainly inhabited by Kandhas.

The district is predominantly inhabited by Scheduled Tribes. They constitute 51.98 per cent to the district's total population as per 2001 Census. Kandhas are the principal Scheduled Tribes found in the district followed by Gonads. Some of the primitive tribes such as Kutia Kandhas, Dongria Kandhas and Mahila Kandhas are found in the remote hill areas of the district. The Kandhas, by nature, are rigid in their ethno-cultural life style and hardly welcome acculturation. Tikabali block which is under study also exhibits the same topography and climate like the district. The demographic picture also shows the high dominance of Kandhas in the block.

Objectives

In this backdrop attempts have been made in the paper to explore the following objectives:

1. To study the socio-economic background of the elected representatives to various Gram Panchayats of the study under review.
2. To explore their capabilities in executing and understanding various schemes.

3. To evaluate the success and failure of the developmental programmes like SGRY and EFC in the regions.
4. To suggest some measures for further policy paradigms.

Methodology

Keeping in view of the objectives of the study, the Tikabali Block in the district of Kandhamala (Orissa) has been selected purposively due to its high tribal concentration. But the finding of study can also be generalized to other parts of the region with the similar background. The study area covers all the 12 Gram Panchayats functioning under Tikabali Panchayat Samiti, data have been collected both from primary and secondary sources in order to analyze the profile of the elected representatives and working of the programmes such as SGRY and EFC. For the collection of primary data questionnaire method with the help of personal interviews have been adopted. As it is extremely difficult to contact all the elected members in their native villages. So the Panchayat functionaries have been contacted in Panchayat Samiti Office at different time intervals by frequent visits. Besides the above method observation method has also been adopted. Official records are used to collect information regarding the actual allotment of funds to various GPs and their effects in the economy. To know about the impact of simple random sampling method, has been interviewed for a clear understanding of the study simple statistical devices like percentage and mean have been used.

Analysis

Attempts have been made in the section to examine the function of GPs in assuring employment and thereby ameliorating poverty in three sub-heads:

(1) Socio-economic profile of the elected members with a linkage to their personality development.

(2) SGRY: Its out-comes and leakages.

(3) EFC: Its civic purpose and benefit received.

Social-economy Background of the Elected Representatives

This part of the study examines male-female-wise and community-wise representation of members to various GPs, level of literacy, economic status, frequency of attending training programmes and the constraints faced by them.

Table1
Male-Female-wise and Community-wise Elected Representatives

Name of G.P.	SC		ST		B.C.		U.R.		Total		G. Total
	M	*F*	*M*	*F*	*M*	*F*	*M*	*F*	*M*	*F*	
1 Tikabali	3	2	7	4	1	1	2	1	13	8	21
2 Beheragaom	4	3	8	5	1	1	2	0	15	9	24
3 Pikaradi	1	-	8	5	1	-	-	1	10	6	16
4 Katimaha	2	2	6	4	-	1	1	-	9	7	16
5 Kainjhar	4	2	8	5	1	1	2	2	15	10	25
6 Badimunda	1	1	4	3	-	1	1	-	6	5	11
7 Gadaguda	2	1	6	4	1	1	2	1	11	7	18
8 Burbinaju	1	1	6	4	1	-	1	1	9	6	15
9 Gandirgia	2	1	6	4	-	1	1	-	9	6	15
10 Paburia	3	2	7	4	-	1	1	-	11	7	18
11 Guttingea	2	2	4	3	1	-	1	-	8	5	13
12 Padangi	1	1	4	3	1	-	1	-	7	4	11
Total	26	18	74	48	8	8	15	6	123	80	203

Table 1 reveals that there are 203 elected members functioning in 12 GPs of Tikabali Block. Out of, 8 are male *sarpanchas*, four are female Sarpanchas and the rest are ward members. As far as male-female wise distribution is concerned the representation of female is 80 (39.41%) and male is 123 (60.59%). Both the ST male (74 Nos) and ST female (48 nos) out number the representation of all communities, Kainjhar Gram Panchayat has the highest (25) number of elected members followed by Padangi and Badimunda having the lowest representation i.e. 11.

Total 2 depicts the literacy position of the elected members. It is found that 39.40% are below 7th class and 46.80% know only their signatures. The ward members are mostly coming under this category, similarly the females are more illiterate then the male members. It is also investigated that more female and less male members are putting their signature only by practice.

Table 2
Levels of Literacy of both Male and Female Members

Educational position	*No. of members*	*Value in %age*
Literacy of male members		
Graduation	2	0.99
Below Graduation but 10th pass	10	4.93
7th and 10th class	16	7.88
Below 7th class	80	39.40
Putting the signature only	95	46.80
Total	203	100.00
Literacy of female members		
Below Graduation but 10th pass	3	3.75
7th to 10th class	10	12.50
Below 7th class	15	18.75
Putting the signature only	52	65.00
Total	80	100.00

The economic status as shown in Table 3 of the elected members so reflect that 83.74% of members are depending upon agriculture followed by 11.33% business and other related activities, similarly a majority of members (59.11%) are the marginal farmers and 33.50% members have lands less then 1 acre. The average monthly income is also not encouraging for the members. 45.81% members have less than 1000 followed by 39.41% members having a monthly income ranging between 1000 4000.

Table 4 reflects that still a major portion of elected members are not attending the training programmes on the ground of economic backwardness and illiteracy.

Table 5 highlights that 37.50% of members are facing problems form their side of husbands and other local politicians. Similarly 18.75% and 31.25% members are facing the problems on the ground lack of confidence and productive and reproductive role respectively.

Table 3
Economic Status of the Members

	No. of members	*Value in %age*
A. Nature of occupation and family background		
Ex-Govt. employees	10	4.93
Agriculture	170	83.74
Businesses and other activities	23	11.33
Total	203	100.00
B. Positions of land-holding		
1 to 5 acres	15	7.39
Less then 1 acres	68	33.50
Marginal farmers	120	59.11
Total	203	100.00
C. Average monthly income		
More than 4000	30	14.78
1000 to 4000	80	39.41
Less than 1000	93	45.81
Total	203	100.00

Table 4
Participation of Women Members in the Training Programmes

Training programmes held	*organized by*	*Total woman members*	*Members Present*	*Present to Total*
October 03	Pallisri (NGO)	80	40	50.00
March 04	Swati (NGO)	80	55	68.75
July 04	DRDA	80	04	5.00
October 04	PD	80	04	5.00

Table 5
Socio-economic Constraints of Women Members

Problems as revealed	*Responds*	*Percent to total*
Productive ad reproductive role (Child bearing)	25	31.25
Lack of confidence	15	18.75
Interference of husbands and deep rooted local politicians	30	37.50
Cultural and religious obstacles	10	12.50
Total	80	100.00

Sampooran Grameen Rozgar Yojana (SGRY)

Government has made an array of interventions in the past for reduction of rural poverty. One such intervention is provision of wage employment for the poor. Several wage employment programmes such as NREP (1980), RLEGP (1983), JRY (1988), EAS (1993), JGSY (1999), have been in operation in the past for rural poor. Sampooran Grameen Rozgar Yojana, a centrally sponsored wage employment programme of the Ministry of Rural Development is latest among them. The programme was launched on 25th September, 2001 with an annual outlay of Rs. 10,000 crores by merging the hitherto on going schemes of the Employment Assurance Scheme (EAS), (the only additional wage employment scheme for rural areas) and the Jawahar Gram Samrdhi Yojana (JGSY) (a rural infrastructure development scheme).

The programme is in operation for more than three years and thousands of crores of rupees have been invested along with millions of tones of food grains during this period. This is the right time to assess the usefulness of the programme in the context of its objectives. This paper is a modest attempt to examine the SGRY in terms of conceptual aspects *vis-à-vis* operational problems cropped up during the implementation.

Rationale

Unemployment, poverty and malnutrition are the main problems of our countryside. These problems are assuming dangerous proportions further due to ever-increasing population, mechanization and contracting job opportunities in rural areas particularly in agriculture, construction, small and medium enterprises sector. In the scenario of declining growth rate of employment increasing number of unemployed, 193.2 million poor people (BPL) living in rural areas, and India being home of nearly 25 per cent world's hungry population despite considerable food surpluses the SGRY assumes importance. Besides generating employment, the programme envisages making a dent on the prevailing poverty and slow growth in the rural economy and to provide food security and demand driven infrastructure at the village level to facilitate faster growth by increasing opportunities of employment through access to the market oriented economy.

Objectives

1. Primarily, the programme aims at providing additional and supplementary wage employment to provide food security and improve nutritional levels in all rural areas.
2. Creation of durable community, social and economic assets and infrastructural development in rural areas is the secondary objective.

The programme is self-targeting in nature and is open to all rural poor, needy of wage employment and desirous of doing the manual and unskilled work.

Strategy

The scheme is implemented on cost sharing basis between the Centre and the States in the ratio of 75 : 25 of the cash component and 100 per cent food grains are provided by the Central Government to the States/UTs free of cost.

The programme is wholly implemented by the Panchayati Raj Institutions (PRIs) i.e. District Panchayats, intermediate Panchayats and Village Panchayats. Resources (funds and food-grains) are made available to all the three tiers of PRIs in the ratio of 20 : 30 : 50, it is ensured that out of 50 per cent of funds, each Gram Panchayat gets minimum Rs. 25,000. Initially implemented in two streams, i.e., stream-I (ZP and PS) and stream-II (GP), from 01 April, 2004 both the streams have been merged into one. Five per cent funds and food-grains under the scheme are retained by the MORD for utilization in the areas of acute distress, arising out of natural preventive measures in the chronically drought or flood affected areas. "Special Component" comprising of only food grains takes care of the states affected by the natural calamity to meet exigencies. While providing wage employment, preference is to be given to agricultural wage earners, non-agricultural unskilled wage earners, marginal farmers. The persons affected by natural calamities, women, members of SCs/STs and parents of child labour withdrawn from hazardous occupation and handicapped children or adult children of handicapped parents who are desirous of working manually.

The trends of funds allocated, released, available and utilised under SGRY-I (EAS) and SGRY-II (JGSY) 2001-02, 2002-03, and 2003-04 in India is depicted in Table 6.

The detailed list of statement showing the defaulting states in releasing their share of funds: stream-I and II SGRY (EAS) and SGRY (JGSY) is from 2001-04 have been illustrated in Table 7.

The detailed list of the food-grains allocated/authorized, lifted and distributed under SGRY-I (EAS) and SGRY-II (JGSY) in 2001-04 mandays generated and number of works completed in stream wise is mentioned in Table 8.

Sampoorna Grameen Rozgar Yojana (SGRY) in Kandhamal District

SGRY is a key programme launched with an aim to generate employment opportunities with the provisions of food security. It is a need based social and economic infrastructure with an ambition of creating man days in lean agriculture seasons. It aims at generation of supplemental wage employment with creation of durable economic infrastructure. The SGRY is a micro approach with an aim to provide additional wage employment in the tribal areas along with creation of social and economic assets. However, it should not be seen merely to provide a social safety net to the downtrodden, in fact it is vast investment in creating human capital and channel sing their potentialities in nation building exercises.

Table 6

Funds Allocated Released, Available and Utilized under SGRY - I (EAS) and SGRY - II (JGSY) 2003-04

Stream	*Allocation (Rs. in lacs)*		*Actual Release (Rs. in lacs)*		*Available including OB & Misc. Receipts*	*Utilization*	*% of Utiliza-tion*
1	*2*		*3*		*4*	*5*	*6*
YEAR 2001-02 AS ON 11.07.2002							
	Central	*State*	*Central Release of Col. 2a*	*State Release of Col. 2b*			
1	*2a*	*2b*	*3a*	*3b*	*4*	*5*	*6*
SGRY-I	187300.00	62373.92	189658.11 (101.26)	51797.92 (83.04)	289038.58	202084.53	69.92
SAGY-II	187060.00	62241.17	189210.70 (101.15)	62976.37 (101.17)	286788.93	217122.43	75.71
Total-a	374360.00	124615.09	378868.81 (101.20)	114774.29 (92.10)	575827.51	419206.96	72.80
Year 2002-03							
SGRY-I	177875.02	59235.26	184753.67 (103.87)	61242.85 (103.39)	333216.71	25498.15	76.47
SGRY-II	177378.00	59021.72	183709.91 (103.57)	58551.09 (99.20)	308221.18	245203.31	79.55

Total-b	355253.02	118256.98	368463.58 (103.72)	119793.94 (101.30)	641437.89	500001.46	77.95
1	2a	2b	3a	3b	4	5	6
Year 2003-04							
SGRY-I	205995.00	68599.66	206156.30 (100.08)	46930.10 (68.41)	336163.40	207386.12	61.69
SGRY-II	206030.00	68555.50	205947.49 (99.96)	48130.14 (70.21)	320293.36	205446.36	64.14
Total-c	412025.00	137155.16	412103.79 (100.60)	95060.28 (69.31)	65456.76	412832.48	62.89
G.Total (a+b+c)	1141638.02	380027.23	1159436.18 (101.60)	329628.51 (86.74)	1870722.16	1332040.90	71.20

Source: Annual Report of MORD (GOI) Years 2002-03 and 2003-04 (figures given in the parentheses indicate percentage).

Table 7
The Defaulting States in Releasing Their Share of Funds: Stream - I and II

Year	*No. of States*	*Stream-I*	*No. of States*	*Stream-2*
2001-02	16	Arunachal Pradesh, A.P. Goa, Assam, Bihar, Gujarat, Himachal Pradesh, Jharkhand, Uttaranchal, WB Karnataka, Maharastra, Manipur, Meghalaya, Nagaland, Punjab	2	Manipur, Meghalaya
2002-03	13	Andhra Pradesh, Arunachal Pradesh, Assam, Goa, Gujarat, Kerala, Manipur, Meghalaya, Nagaland, Orissa, Tripura, Uttaranchal, WB.	11	Arunachal Pradesh, Assam, Goa, Gujarat, Haryana, Himachal Pradesh, Manipur, Meghalaya, Nagaland, Orissa, Punjab Uttaranchal, WB.
2003-04	19	Andhra Pradesh, Arunachal Pradesh, Assam, Bihar, Chattisgarh, Goa, Gujarat, Himachal Pradesh Jharkhand, Karnataka, Kerela, MP, Maharashtra, Manipur, Meghalaya, Nagaland, Punjab, UP, WB.	22	Andhra Pradesh, Arunachal Pradesh, Assam, Bihar, Goa, Gujarat, Haryana, Himachal Pradesh, Jharkhand, Karnataka, Kerela, MP, Manipur, Meghalaya, Mizoram, Nagaland, Punjab, Sikkim, UP. WB.

Source: Annual Report of MORD (GOI) Year 2002-03 and 2003-04.

Table 8

Food-grains Allocated/Autorized, Lifted and Distributed under SGRY-1 (EAS) & SGRY-II (JGSY) 2001-2004 Mandays Generated and Number of Works Completed

Stream	*Allocated (tonnes)*	*Authorisation*	*Lifted tonnes*	*% of Col. 3*	*Distribute Tonne*	*% of Col. 3*	*Mandays generated*	*No. of works completed*
1	*2*	*3*	*4*	*5*	*6*	*7*	*8*	*9*
Year 2001-02 (upto 11-07-2002)								
SGRY-I	1692640		-				2605540	170928
SAGY-II	1756350	-	-				2624240	936261
Total-a	3448990	-	-				5229780	1107189
Year 2002-03								
SGRY-I	2250000	3057510	2645740	60.26	1746980	66.03	3811480	414465
SGRY-II	2250000	2917080	2512530	86.66	1850960	73.67	3671450	1001631
Total-b	4500000	5955660	5158270	86.59	3597940	69.75	7482930	1416096
Year 2003-04								
SGRY-I	2250000	3057510	2645740	60.26	1746980	66.03	3811480	414465
SGRY-II	2250000	2917080	1931270	66.21	1691510	87.59	3233170	614997
Total-c	4500000	5955660	3721850	62.49	3286000	88.30	6374490	1046589
G.Total b+c	12448990	11912490*	8880120*	74.54*	6883940*	77.52	19087200#	3569874#

Source: Annual Report of MORD (GOI) Year 2002-03 and 2003-04.

* Total of the years 2002-03 & 2003-04. # Total of the years 2001-02 & 2003-04.

It is a promise to provide at least hundred days employment in lean agriculture seasons particularly those who are below the poverty line (BPL). It also creates substantial scopes for land less agriculture workers to earn their minimum livelihood, so it has a paramount importance more particularly in tribal areas to tackle poverty at social level. The trend of allotment of funds for various GPs from 2000-05 have been in Table 9.

Table 9
Allotment of funds and Rice from 2000-05 to GPs

Sl. No.	*Name of G.P.*	*Allotment of funds (in Rs.)*	*Rice (in Qt.)*
For the session 2004-05 (up to Dec 2005)			
1	Tikabali	280164	335
2	Gadaguda	206421	247
3	Pikaradi	236355	282
4	Badimunda	151403	181
5	Paburia	303488	363
6	Guttingia	281556	336
7	Padangi	137097	163
8	Katimaha	225894	270
9	Gandirgia	171468	204
10	Kainjhar	358137	428
11	Beheragaom	291467	348
12	Burbinaju	264613	316
	Total	2908063	3473
For the session 2003-04			
1	Tikabali	428577	382
2	Gadaguda	315771	281
3	Pikaradi	361564	322
4	Badimunda	231608	207
5	Paburia	464260	414
6	Guttingia	430709	384
7	Padangi	209722	187
8	Katimaha	345561	308
9	Gandirgia	262303	234
10	Kainjhar	547858	489
11	Beheragaom	445871	397
12	Burbinaju	404719	361
	Total	4448595	3966

Sl. No.	*Name of G.P.*	*Allotment of funds (in Rs.)*	*Rice (in Qt.)*
For the session 2002-03			
1	Tikabali	556295	498
2	Gadaguda	409873	368
3	Pikaradi	469311	420
4	Badimunda	300628	270
5	Paburia	602610	542
6	Guttingia	59063	502
7	Padangi	272218	245
8	Katimaha	448538	402
9	Gandirgia	340469	305
10	Kainjhar	711119	637
11	Beheragaom	578738	519
12	Burbinaju	525417	472
	Total	5774279	5180
For the session 2001-02			
1	Tikabali	407431	397
2	Gadaguda	300189	292
3	Pikaradi	343724	335
4	Badimunda	220179	214
5	Paburia	41352	429
6	Gutingia	608832	593
7	Padangi	*	*
8	Katimaha	328509	319
9	Gandirgia	249361	242
10	Kainjahr	520823	507
11	Beheragaom	423870	413
12	Burbinaju	384816	375
	Total	4229086	4116

Padangi G.P. was not created.

Table 9 clearly highlight that there has been disproportionate and disparity with allocation of funds to certain GPs. It is found that the GPs in serial No. 10 and 15 are getting more shares of funds and GPs in serial No. 9, 4 and 7 are receiving less amounts of allotments similarly it is found that a major portion of money under this extension scheme has been for the purpose of construction of rest-sheds, village roads, extension of school building, small culverts, prayer halls, renovation of ponds, tank etc. But it is noticed that the quality of work dine under SGRY is not up to satisfaction. There is a wide gap between the amount of money released and the quantity of works done.

A huge portion of money goes to the pockets of elected representatives and official in the way of corruption, the illegal nexus between the contractors and Panchayat functionaries cause misuse of founds at the bottom level. There is also a huge complain of non-consultation with village headman and members of Gram Sabha by the *sarapanch* as while preparing the Action Plans for various project. Sometimes work estimation are wrongly prepared and fake utilization certificates are submitted by the Panchayat heads. It is also found that to spend the allocated funds in a stipulated period works done hurriedly and projects are selected improperly by ignoring the collective interests of the masses.

Eleventh Finance Commission (EFC)

This scheme was launched in the year 2000 for a period of five years. The main aim of this programme is to provide minimum civic amenities to the people in the from of social sector development. The major thrust areas under this scheme are primary health, primary education, safe drinking water, village sanitation, maintenance of public property and street lighting. The fund sharing under EFC between the central government and the State Government is 75 : 25. It is found from the official records that all the GPs have been sanctioned equal amounts of founds that is Rs. 95,00 (Central share) and Rs. 23, 750 (States share) except Tikabali GP. Tikabali GP is qualified to receive Rs. 1,10,000 and Rs. 27500 as its population exceeds 5000, like other programme serious loopholes and bottlenecks have been found in the implementation of founds by the Panchayat authorities, in some case expenditures have also been elected wrong.

Findings

1. It is found in the matters of personality development the women representatives show their apathy to attend the meetings because of poor economic backgrounds and illiteracy (Table 4).
2. The women representatives still face considerable handicaps to their involvement in politics because of reproductive and reproductive rules, lack of self-confidence and opposition of entrenched cultural and religious views (Table 5).
3. Unnecessary interference of their husbands, deep rooted politicians and villages level leaders also discourage the women representatives in performing their responsibilities rightly (Table 5).
4. Bureaucratic and administrative complicacy also result in less understanding regarding the implementation and execution of the programmes.
5. It is observed that the low income status of elected representatives also become a stumbling block in the way of their taking up the responsibilities in Panchayats (Table 2).
6. As far as SGRY is concerned, in the basis of opinions of the beneficiaries, it is found that there is a wide range of gap between mandays created officially and man-days created actually.
7. Several respondents view that rice supplied in SGRY Scheme are not properly distributed because of corruption at the contractor level.
8. It is observed that Social Audit is done only in pen and paper which leads to misuse of funds by both officials and politicians.
9. It is seen that some less feasible projects have been taken because of either absence of village level committies or non-consultation with members by the Sarapanchas.
10. The funds under EFC are misutilised by the Panchayat functionaries to give better civic facilities in their own streets and villages ignoring the common interests.

11. The state share of 25% to EFC is not matched in time.
12. Under SGRY sub-standard quality of rice are supplied as viewed by most of the beneficiaries.

Conclusions

A perusal of the study clearly demonstrate that tribal people needs to be educated and awareness are to be created in order to reap the real benefits from the PRIs. Suitable amendments should be made in the floor of legislature to punish the dishonest official and plug the loopholes in the proper implementation of the need-based development programmes in tribal areas. PRIs, particularly in tribal region, should be strengthened with such legal and legislative power so that can continue to play a vital role in creating a socio-economic in change in tribal Indian. Hence, in order to accelerate the process of promoting the right of the tribal people in all walks of life, it is essential to galvanise the PRIs with more functional, financial and administrative autonomy. Greater devolution of powers in favour of PRIs in turn with 73rd Constitutional Amendment Act and Article 243(G) of Constitution of India can help these institutions to mobilize poverty socially by creating conducive income and employment opportunities. Thus, in various facets of tribal development, PRIs through Grama Sabha can prove themselves as potent instrument in mobilizing the resources, creating employment opportunities, ensuring food security, enhancing the level of awareness about the scheme, promoting transparency in the implementation of the programme, encouraging people's partnership, ensuring accountability, creditability and sustain-ability in development. At various level government attempts have been taken quit seriously during and immediately after independence. But, the saddest part of the stay i.e. we are yet nukes a way to reach even nearer to the point of tribal development. To conclude, as the tribal economies have too many contradictions and also need to be resolved, so PRIs with its profound impact can play an integrative role in driving the dormant resources in most productive paths.

REFERENCES

Bailey, F.G., *Tribe Cast and Nation: A Study of Political Activity and Political Change in High Land Orissa*, 1900.

Bhurye, G.S., *The Scheduled Tribes*, 2nd Edition. Bombay, 1959.

District Statistical Handbook - Kandhamal, 1999, Directorate of Economics and Statistics, Government of Orissa, Bhubaneswar.

Mahi, Pal, "Capacity Building of Zilla Parishad Functionaries", *Kurukshetra*, Vol-52, No-5, March 4.

Panchayat Samiti, *Tikabali* (GP Section, S.K. Patnaik)

Panda, G.C., "Development of Tribe Women through Self-Help Groups: A Study in Kandhamal District", paper presented in an UGC National Conference (8-10 Aug, 2004), Nagarjuna University, Guntur, A.P.

Panda, G.C., Empowering Tribal Women through SHGs: A Study in Kandhamal district" paper presented in an UGC State Level Conference (12-13 Sept, 2004), UNS College, Khairabada, Mugpal, Jajpur, Orissa.

Panda, G.C. and Tripathy, S., "Impact of Road Transport on Population: A study in Kandhamal District, Orissa." In: *Problems of Population in India*, Panigrahy, R.L. (ed), Discovery Publishing House, New Delhi, 2004.

Panigrahy, R.L., *Human Resource Development and Labour Welfare*, Mohit Publishers, New Delhi, 2002.

Panigrahy, R.L., "Women Empowerment in Policy and Politics", Presented in UGC Seminar in Kalinga Mahavidyalaya, G. Udayagiri, Dec, 2001.

Pilai, Sudha, Can Panchayati Raj improve the Scene?, *Yojana*, Vol. 45, Aug 1.

Roy Burman, B.K., *A Preliminary Appraisal of the Scheduled Tribes India*, Office of the Registrar General, Government of India, New Delhi, 1969.

Sharma, K.R., "A Study of Educational Backwardness of Tribal Students", *The Educational Quarterly*, April 1983.

Singh, Puran, SGRY and Employment Generation: An assessment, *Kurukshetra*, Vol. 53, No. 10, Aug, 05.

Sinha, Archana, "Women in Local Self Governance", *Kurukshetra*, Vol 52, No. 10, August 4, 3.

Smaranika Kandhamala Mohouchhaba 2003: District Council of Culture, Kandhamal District, Phulbani.

Tripathy, S.N., "Education for tribal women". In: *Tribal Women in India*, Tripathy, S.N. (ed.), Mohit Publications, New Delhi, 2002.

7

Revitalisation of Panchayats

Dr. B. Eswar Rao Patnaik*

Introduction

India can not march on the path to progress and prosperity, unless rural areas are developed. Panchayati Raj Institutions are completing 48 years of inception in India. Sukracharya in ancient times has advocated the institution of village councils (*panchayats*), in his work *Neeti Sasthra* in India. Panchayati Raj Institution seems to have developed from the welcome suggestions of Sri Balwant Rai Mehta, the Chairman of the Committee (1957), that probed into the functioning of CDP and NES and suggested measures for achieving economy and efficiency in their implementation. The committee has spelled out that, wastage of colossal amounts of expenditure and dismal failure of CDP to evoke public response have rendered the experiments, CDP and NES, a frustrated one. Consistent with the Article 40 of the Constitution, the Committee has recommended the formulation of Village Panchayats, Panchayat Samities and Zilla Parishad at village, block and district levels, respectively. The creation of Panchayati Raj Institutions in line with a three-tier structure was accepted by National Development Council, debated in Parliament and the planners and public authorities of the country have substituted the words "Panchayati Raj" for the name democratic decentralisation.

The earliest starters in launching Panchayati Raj Institutions in India were Rajasthan and Andhra Pradesh

* Reader in Economics and HOD, S.B.R.G. Womens' College, Berhampur (Gm.), Orissa.

(October, 1959). The three-tier structure was experimented in states, like Andhra Pradesh, Bihar, Gujarat, Karnataka, Himachal Pradesh, Madhya Pradesh, Maharashtra, Punjab, Rajasthan; Tamil Nadu, Uttar Pradesh, West Bengal, Arunachal Pradesh and Chandigarh. In the remaining states and Union Territories, wither a two-tier or a one structure was followed.

The Rational behind Local Governance

Panchayati Raj Institutions will be vibrant institutions performing necessary developmental, regulatory and general administrative functions. Amartya Sen visualises that, development consists in expansion of choices of people of a country and strong Panchayati Raj Institutions, facilitate the expansion of peoples choices. Rajiv Gandhi has foreseen Panchayat institutions as instruments for rural uplift.

Jean Dreze and Amartya Sen, authors of *India: Economic Development and Social Opportunity*, plead that "many of the public provisions that have to be made in order to promote basic equality and ensure minimum social security involve local public services, participation (of people) has intrinsic value of quality of life. It is no eight wonder, of the world that, the development-oriented eight and ninth five year plans in India have assigned over-riding priority for development of participatory institution, like Panchayati Raj.

Contemporary Indian Situation

Data analysis of Indian economy, as per the 2001 census, reveals that, only 51.805 of households at country level have permanent houses, 39.0% of population have safe drinking water facility by sources, like, tap/pump, within the premises of the house, 43.52% of Indians only use electricity as a source of lighting and nearly 22.83% of households have bathroom in their houses. The dark spot in the body of the economy is that, only 31.49% of households in the poor economy of India possess assets like radio, TV, telephone and bicycles. A vast segment of populations in India suffer from grinding poverty (26%) and it is a sad commentary on plan performances at country level that, merely 35.5% of population in the country avail facilities of Banking services. So, efforts may be made at country level to transform the sad picture of India into a rosy one by creating vibrant Panchayati Raj Institutions.

Gandhian Version of Panchayats

Villages are the arteries of India. Mahatma Gandhi in his work *Rebuilding Our Villages* believes that, Panchayat has to promote education of its boys and girls, its sanitation, its medical needs of upkeep and cleanliness of village ponds, uplift and fulfilment of wants of its so-called untouchables. Gandhi has advocated dispersal of power as maintained by him "independence must begin at the bottom. Thus, every village will be a panchayat having fill powers. In this structure composed of innumerable villages, there will be ever widening never ascending circles. Life will not be a pyramid with the apex sustained by the bottom."

Structure of Panchayats

There is a wealth of wisdom in the editorial observation of *Kurukshetra* (June 1993) that, the 72nd Amendment Bill, 1991 can rightly be described as an epoch-making event in the history of democratic decentralisation in the country. It is the realisation of the dreams of our forefathers and it may enable the poor and deprived to have their rightful place in the process of development. The 72nd Amendment Bill 1991 which was passed in Lok Sabha on 22 December, 1992 was approved by Rajya Sabha and President of India latter.

Embodied below are the salient features of the Seventy-third Amendment Act, 1992:

(a) The Gram Sabha comprises all the members registered as voters in the Panchayat areas.

(b) The Panchayati Raj has a three-tier structure of Panchayat at village intermediate and district levels.

(c) Seats in Panchayat at all the three levels shall be filled by direct election. Further, chairpersons of Village Panchayats can be made members of Panchayats at district levels. M.Ps., M.L.As. and M.L.Cs. could also be members of Panchayats at district level.

(d) One redeeming feature of Panchayats is reservation of seats for S.Cs. and S.Ts. in proportion to their population in the state and it is a ray of hope for the women to secure reservation of one third total sets for them.

(e) Offices of the Chairpersons of the Panchayats at all levels shall be reserved in favour of S.Cs. and S.Ts. in proportion to their population in the state. One-third office of Chairpersons of Panchayats shall be reserved for women.

(f) State legislature shall have the liberty to provide reservation of seats and offices of chairperson of Panchayats in favour of other backward class citizens.

(g) Every Panchayat will have a uniform five-year term and in case of dissolution, election will be compulsorily held within six months.

(h) It will not be possible to dissolve the existing Panchayats by amendment of any constitution before the expiry of its duration.

(i) A person who is disqualified under any law for elections to the legislature of the state shall not be eligible to become a member of Panchayat.

(j) For superintendence, direction and control of the electoral process and preparation of electoral rolls an independent Election Commission will be constituted.

(k) The responsibility for implementation of development schemes for development and social justice in respect of matters enlisted in Eleventh Schedule shall be entrusted to the Panchayat.

(l) To be able to perform various functions efficiently, the Panchayats will receive grants from state government and a portion of revenue of certain taxes levied by the state government. In some cases, Panchayats will be permitted to collect and retain revenue it raises.

(m) In each state a Finance Commission will be established within one year and then after every five years to determine the principles on the basis of which adequate financial resources would be ensured for Panchayat.

(n) The Panchayat existing on 24 April, 1993 will be allowed to complete their full term, unless dissolved by the house by resolution.

Spectrum of Activities of Panchayats

The Government of India has vested the development of the following areas of enterprise to Panchayats, as envisaged in Eleventh Schedule (Article 243G). Agriculture land improvement, implementation of land reforms, consolidation and soil conservation, minor irrigation and watershed development, animal husbandry, dairying and poultry farming, fisheries, social forestry, minor forest produce, small scale industries, khadi, village and cottage industries, rural housing, drinking water, fuel and fodder, roads, bridges, ferries and water ways, rural electrification, non-conventional energy sources, poverty eradication programmes, education, technical training and vocational education, adult and non-formal education, libraries, cultural activities markets and fairs, health and sanitation, family welfare, women and children, social welfare including welfare of the handicapped and mentally retarded and welfare of S.Cs. and S.Ts are some thrust areas of attention of the Panchayats.

Defects in the Working Panchayats

Panchayati Raj was carefully nurtured by Pandit Nehru. However, these institutions were cut down in size by his successors. The Panchayati Raj Institutions have witnessed (i) the phase of ascendancy (1959-65), (ii) the phase of stagnation (1965-69) and (iii) the phase of decline from 1969 onwards, in recent years, there is some effort at official levels to revitalise panchayts at country level. The Ashok Mehta Committee on Panchayati Raj (1978) has succinctly observed that "Panchayati Raj Institutions are dominated by economically and socially privileged sections of society and have as such facilitated the emergence of oligarchic forces yielding no benefits to weaker sections. The performance of Panchayati Raj Institutions have been vitiated by political factionalism rather than development thrust. Corruption, inefficiency, scant regard for procedures, political interference in day to day administration, parochial locality, motivated actions, power concentration instead of service consciousness, all these have seriously limited the utility of Panchayati Raj. As observed out be Sitaram Singh (1986), people who run panchayats have not received training to make them conversant with their responsibilities and the bureaucratic response to change and development is not up to the expectations.

Suggestions

In the revitalisations process, the following aspects may be considered.

To enforce people's entitlement to participation, acts should stipulate for quarterly meetings of Gram Sabha to discuss vital matters and implement them. Efforts may be made to conduct Panchayat elections compulsorily once in every five years and these ought to be conducted by Chief Election Commissioner of the State. Plan endeavour may embark on strengthening Village Panchayat, village co-operatives and village schools and women youth and farmers may be linked with development of these institutions, public authorities should provide sufficient funds to Panchayats to accelerate development and the Panchayats should tap rural sector for raising funds. Education of rural adult population is crucial for the success of institutional development and study camps, group discussions, TV Programmes and peoples participation in Panchayat institutions are requirements of the day.

Conclusion

To conclude, the scale of endeavour may be raised by sensible bureaucrat social workers, people, NGO's, implementing agencies and youth. Property may be seen as an instrument of service and poverty will be eliminated to the extent that Governance improves.

Acknowledgement

The article is dedicated to the memory of my sister late B. Vimala Devi, Sr. Lecturer in Political sciences, Womens College, Jeypore discussions with whom has sharpened my thought.

REFERENCES

Drez, Jean and Amartya Sen, *India: Economic Development and Social Opportunity*.

Gandhi, M.K., *Rebuilding Our Villages*.

Government of India, 2001, Census.

Prime Minister writers to all sarpanches, *Kurukshetra*, June 1993.

Singh, Sitaram, "Revitalisation of Panchayats", *Kurukshetra*, April, 1986.

8

Indira Awas and PRI (Housing for Rural Poor)

Dr. Bishnu Narayan Sethi*

Look of terurial rights, speculative land market in flexible housing finance system, in appropriate planning and building regulations, ignorance about the cost and energy effective construction technologies and look to institutional framework for supporting the poor are some of the hurdles in tacking the rural housing problem. The withdrawal of the state from social sectors is also a major policy deviation that hinders the enabling and facilitating role.

The National Housing and Habitat Policy has given special emphasis to the involvement and participation of the Panchayati Raj Institution (PRIs) and the women in providing shelter to the shelterless. The Seventy-third Amendment to the Constitution says that the PRIs shall prepare plans for economic development and social justice at their levels including 29 subjects listed in the Eleventh Schedule of the constitution. As per this list the subject Rural Housing has been given to the PRIs.

Poverty reflects the ability of an individual to satisfy certain minimum needs for a sustained healthy and a reasonably productive living shelter and quality of housing in one of the basic needs of an individual for the participation in the social development process which will lead to reduction of poverty. Housing is considered as fundamental right. Several initiatives have been taken by the United Nations Centre for Human

* Lecturer of Economics in L.N. Degree College, Kodala, Ganjam, Orissa and Research Fellow, ICSSR, New Delhi.

Settlement to Eradicate Homelessness which is a state of deprivation. 1987 was declared as the International Year of shelter for the Homeless (IYSH). A global shelter strategy was formulated with the goal of houses for all by the year 2001. In spite of the declaration, summits and seminars, the problem remains unsolved. It is appropriate at this juncture to look at the housing scenario in our country.

Shelter and development are complementary and supplementary to each other. Provision of shelter has been one of the critical components of the governments strategy for employment generation and poverty alleviation in rural areas since the beginning of the planning era in the country. In November, 1988 the United Nations had called upon all the Governments of he world to formulate their respective National Housing Policies. According to the Government of India had adopted the National Housing Policy in 1994 for the formation of this sector. Subsequently concern was shown for habitat development in the wake of the Habitat Conferences convened by the United Nations at Istanbul (Turkey) in 1996. The Istanbul Declaration was a commitment on the part of the global community to create for every human being a sustainable habit covering all the aspects of man in relation to nature.

Later in the context of the process of liberalization, privatization and globalization (LPG), it was thought necessary to re-articulate the National Housing Policy for establishing partnership with various stake-holders including the private sector, the community, the voluntary sector etc. In more concrete sense, emphasis was given to widening the meaning of shelter which inter alia, includes provision of adequate sites and services for houses availability of local sources of energy and a healthy environment around the sites. In nut-shell the National Housing and Habitat Policy, 1998 which includes, many others, a shift from a subsidy based housing scheme to a cost sharing one, shift of rural housing strategies from target-orientation to demand-driven empowering the Panchayati Raj Institutions (PRIs) and village co-operatives to mobilize credit for adding to the stock to existing basic amenities in the rural areas modernizing the housing sector in order to enhance its efficiency, productivity, etc., forgoing partnership with private, public, and co-operative sectors in order to increase capacity of the construction industry in the sphere of housing and habitat; involvement and participation of women at all levels of decision-making and enabling them to formulate and implement housing policies and programmes, development of the villages in a manner which provides for a healthy environment increased used of renewable energy sources and pollution free atmosphere with a concern for solid waste disposal, provide quality and cost-effective housing and shelter options to all citizens, particularly the marginalized groups and ensuring that all housing units have easy access to drinking water and sanitation.

Government Programmes

The Government of India announced and National Housing and Habitat Policy in the year 1998 which aimed at providing Housing for all and facilitating the construction of 20 lakh additional housing units (13 lakh in rural area and 7 lakh in urban areas) annually, with emphasis on extending benefits to the poor and the deprived. An action plan had also been prepared, but the action plan more or less remained on paper. The action plan had the following components:

(1) Conversion of unserviceable *kutcha* houses in Indira Awas Yojana.

(2) Pradhan Mantri Gramadaya Yojana Gramin Areas.

(3) Credit-cum-Subsidy scheme for Rural housing.

(4) Samagra Awas Yojana.

(5) Innovative stream for rural housing and Habitat Development.

(6) Rural Building Centres.

(7) Enhancement of equity contribution by ministry of Rural Development to HUDCO.

(8) National mission for Rural Housing and Habitat.

As per the provisional estimates made available under the Indira Awas Yojana (IAY) for the past three years on an average about 14-15 lakh houses are being constructed every years against the annual requirement of about 30 lakh houses. It implies that only 50 per cent of the requirement is being met. In addition to this, it is estimated that about 10 lakh shelter less households are added every year. Thus out of the total requirement 40 lakh units annually, only 15 lakh houses are being constructed, leaving a gap of about 25 lakh houses every year in rural areas.

In the context of the exposition of this housing policy and the nature and extent of the problem of shelter in rural areas, it is proposed to examine the implementation of rural housing scheme particularly IAY and to ascertain as to what extent, the PRI have played their role in proper and effective implementation of the scheme. It is also significant to examine as to how these institutions themselves can mitigate the problem of shelter by mobilizing their own financial and non-financial resources in this regard. This has become more important in the context of the National Common Minimum Programme Agenda of the UPA Government which says that Housing for the weaker sections in rural areas will be expanded in a large scale.

Looking towards future: Creating an enabling environment with effective partnership between verities of Government not only to get the houses on the ground but also to give meaning to the notion of a people centred development should be done. Right from the Central Government down to the Gram Panchayat, including State Government, District Panchayats and Block Panchayats should be the main partner in this process. The Gram Panchayat should be empowered by providing funds, functions and functionaries to be the implementing aim for solving the rural housing problem.

The strategy for developing rural housing would have to be distinctly different from that of urban housing, this is because, inter- and intra-regional variations in the rural areas are far more significant then in urban areas. Keeping in view the need for a more realistic assessment of the housing requirements and the local variations and typology of housing in different parts of the country, a major housing enumeration work is to be carried out with the active involvement and participation of Gram Panchayats. The data obtained through the enumeration has to be analyzed to get the under mentioned informations:

(1) the families having land and no habitable house.

(2) The families having no land and house.

(3) The families whose houses can be made livable by making some repairs and renovations.

(4) Families who can save at least Rs. 5/- per day for house construction.

Rural Housing - The Duty of Gram Panchayat

The National Housing and Habitat Policy has given special emphasis to the involvement and participation of PRIs and the women in providing shelter to the shelter less. The Seventy-third Amendment to the Constitution says that the PRIs shall prepare plans for economic development and social justice at their levels including 29 subjects listed in the Eleventh Schedule of the constitution. As per this list the rural housing subject has been given to the PRIs. In other words, while preparing plans for economic development and social justice panchayats shall also keep in view the status of shelter as well as the status of the entire habitat of the village. As far as the requirement of decision-making by the women is concerned, it may be noted that already one-third seats for the members and the chair persons have been reserved for women at all the three tiers of the PRIs. In the wake of this provision more than one million women have become members and chair persons of these bodies across the countries.

As per the guidelines of the IAY the Zilla Panchayats, District Rural Development Agencies (DRDAs) shall on the basis of the allocations made and targets fixed, decide the number of houses to be constructed/upgraded Panchayat wise under the scheme during a particular financial year. The same shall be intimated to the Gram Panchayat concerned. There after the Gram Sabha (GS) which consists of the all voters of the Gram Panchayat, will select the beneficiaries from the list of eligible below poverty line (BPL) households restricting this number to the target allocated as per the programme guidelines. Selection by the GS is final. No approval by the higher body is required. Zilla Parishad, DRDAs and Block Development Offices should, however, be sent a list of the selected beneficiaries for their information. The priority in the selection of beneficiaries will be as follows:

* Freed bonded labourers.
* S.C/S.T households.
* S.C/S.T households who are victims of atrocity.
* S.C/S.T households headed by widows and unmarried women.
* S.C/S.T households affected by floods, natural calamities like earth quake, cyclone and man made calamities like riots.
* Other S.C/S.T households.
* Non-S.C/S.T BPL households
* Physically and mentally challenged persons.
* Ex-serviceman and retired members of the paramilitary forces; and
* Displaced persons on account of development projects nomadic/semi-nomadic and de-notified tribals, families with physically/mentally challenged members.

The selection of beneficiaries will be subject to the condition that the households of all the above categories except those families/widows of personnel from defence services/para military forces killed in action are in the BPL category. Another important feature of the scheme is that the beneficiaries should be involved in construction of their house. In other words, the beneficiaries may make their arrangement for procurement of construction material, engage skilled workman and also contribute family labour. The beneficiaries will have complete freedom as to the manner of construction of the houses. The allotment of dwelling unit should be in the name of female member of the beneficiary household, alternatively, it can be allotted in the name of both husband and wife. The unit cost for construction of IAY house and up-gradation is given in the Table 1.

An evaluation of the Indira Awas Yojana has been conducted by the Ministry of Rural Development besides other institutions. Let us discuss the salient findings of these evaluations and studies having relevance to the role of PRI in its implementation.

Table 1
The Unit Cost for Construction of IAY House and Up-gradation

Particulars	*Plain area*	*Hilly/Difficult areas*
Construction of house including sanitary, latrine and smokeless *chulha*.	Rs. 25,000	Rs. 27,500
Up-gradation of unserviceable houses.	Rs. 12,500	Rs. 12,500

Evaluation of the Concept

There are many positive features of the implementation of the scheme, e.g.:

* The scheme has been able to provide shelter benefits to a significant proportion of the marginalised groups.
* Gram Sabha (GS) have been involved in the selection of the beneficiaries to a large extent.
* Occupancy rate is very high, most of the houses have been constructed by using local materials with local skills and resources; and
* Houses barring a mini scale proportion have easy access to drinking water with facilities like hand-pumps or village wells.

In general all beneficiaries are satisfied with the constructed houses. But there are a number of areas of concern too, which have emerged from the evolution.

As per the guidelines of the scheme all the beneficiaries under it should be below poverty line. But the evolution study revealed that as many as 36.99% beneficiaries were from families living above the poverty line. In a number of states ineligible families, who get benefits under the scheme, were much higher then the national average, for example, such families were 79.64% in Punjab, 77.66% in Himachal Pradesh, 68.40% in Rajasthan, 67.26% in Maharashtra and 57.00% in Mizoram.

Also the beneficiaries should be selected by the GS only. But the evaluation study revealed that only 78.16% of the beneficiaries were selected by the GS and out of the rest, 12.67% were selected by Government Officials, 5.70% by the M.P/M.L.A. or public representatives.

From the above, it emerges that the selection of the beneficiaries under the scheme was not done properly, if we leave aside 22% selected by others, the rest which were selected by the GS should have been at least from the BPL families. But that was no so clearly, PRIs particularly Gram Panchayats have not played their role as they should have. Hence, it becomes important that in order to give benefits to the deserving families, the meetings of the GS should be held as indicated in the State Panchayat Acts and only the eligible families should get the benefits of the scheme.

Findings

Some impact assessment studies were also conducted by the ministry with the assistance of reputed institutions, the main findings of the studies conducted in the states of Orissa, Haryana, Punjab, U.P. are given below:

* An impact study in Ganjam District of Orissa revealed that the Ward Member presiding the Gram Sabha and the participants villagers were select the beneficiaries of IAY.
* An impact study in Fetehabad District of Haryana revealed that the Sarapanch Acts as a forwarding authority for application forms and no priority is fixed for providing IAY houses. Every thing is in the hands of Block Officials, whosoever satisfies them receives the benefits.
* A study of IAY in Hashipur District revealed that assistance had been given normally in three installment by the installment amount varied.
* A study of IAY of the Chamba District of Himachal Pradesh revealed that in majority of panchayats, the selection is still controlled by Pradhan, Up-Pradhan and secretaries which is evident from the findings that out to the total beneficiaries 46 per cent were selected by Panchayats and 54 per cent by the block development officials. People are ignorant about the scheme and the process of selection of the beneficiaries is out of the hands of the Gram Sabha.

* A study of the scheme of Gonda District indicates that in the infrastructurally developed Blocks 83 per cent of the beneficiaries have been selected by the GS where as in the poorer blocks, the proportion of those selected by the GS is about 69 per cent.

The main findings of the concurrent evaluation and impact assessment studies of the IAY reveal that the panchayats have not been playing their role effectively in the implementation of the scheme.

Future Plan of Action

Then local level habited and housing plan should be formulated by Gram Panchayats in order to facilitate different groups mentioned above to have livable, lovable and affordable houses with in the next plan periods.

That strategy should have the following actions:-

1. Making land available for housing and ensuring tenurial rights.
2. Mobilising credit by encouraging thrift and savings of the poor people and establishing community based housing financial institutions.
3. Encouraging community action by framing self-help groups.
4. Providing technical guidance and support to communities on cost and energy effective construction technologies and materials.
5. Establishing housing environment.
6. Establishing subsidy scheme to provide housing opportunities to the poorest segment,
7. Integrating housing programmes of all tiers of Government and departments with the local level housing plan.
8. Establishing marketing network of building materials.
9. Framing multi-technician groups of crafts man and construction workers and encouraging women to be the members of the group.

10. Creating strategic partnerships and alliances to make the plan work.
11. Gender equity should be maintained in the entire process.

In short the rural housing programme should be a peoples movement with government support. Policies and programmes should be focused to encourage in increasing space for the poor people to improve their living conditions.

Suggestions

Shelter and development are complementary and supplementary to each other. Provision of shelter has been one of the critical components of the government strategy for employment generation and poverty alleviation in rural areas since the beginning of the planning era in the country.

Under the goal of shelter for all the government proposes to end shelterlessness in rural areas by extending benefits to the poor and the deprived. Under IAY 114.17 lakh houses have been constructed by incurring and expenditure about Rs. 19,915.93 crores. But looking at the status of the implementation of the scheme as revealed by the concurrent evaluation of the scheme about 40 per cent of the benefit has been cornered by the undeserving families. If this scopage is not checked a large number of scarce resources will go down the drain. Hence there is need for effective involvement of the PRIs not only in the implementation of the rural housing scheme being sponsored by the Central and State Governments but also in investing its own resources in this sector. This can be done by acting on the following suggestions:

1. There is an urgent need to create awareness about rural housing, particularly on the implementation of the IAY among the selected representatives of PRIs at district and sub-district levels in order to enable these leaders to use the allocated resources under the scheme for deserving people in the villages.
2. The meeting of the Gram Sabha (GS) should be held as prescribed in the Panchayati Raj Acts and according to rules and regulations formulated in this context. It has been observed that meeting of the GS were held

merely as formality as the *sarpanch* and *gram sachiv* rarely took interest in this regard. The beneficiaries under the IAY must be identified by this body only. There is no provision for the selection of beneficiaries by any other agency or bureaucrats or M.Ps/M.L.As. It has been noticed from the findings of the study that the Block Development Officer has real say in the selection of the beneficiaries whereas as per the guidelines of the scheme he is merely required to be intimated by the Gram Panchayats about the progress made in the construction of the houses in his jurisdiction.

To ensure the meeting of the GS it is suggested that a block level Gazetted Officer, who is not from the Panchayati Raj Department may be nominated as observer of the meeting. If the meeting of the GS are held systematically with the maximum participation of villagers genuine beneficiaries will automatically be identified by it.

3. As per Article 243-G of the Constitution, Panchayats are required to prepare plans for economic development and social justice at their levels with some exceptions here and there, the panchayat have neither been preparing nor implementing these plans. Panchayats must begin to take initiative in this context. One of the impact assessment studies of the Hoshiarpur District of Punjab rightly observed "No attempts has been made to plan community level habitat and integrate this with overall rural development programmes". Whilst a few houses are made upgraded household and community waste is accumulating around every village causing not only run off population but ground water contamination. The planning for rural settlement should be for development of rural habitat with focus on shelter. The planning in this context may inter alia, include habitat improvement with focus in rural water supply, drainage, sanitation and village roads. The scheme of rural housing may be implemented in the cluster of villages keeping in view

their population and distance thresholds. Such plan may be taken up in stages so that the entire village may be covered with in specified period of Five-year Plan.

Such an approach to rural housing and habitat development was discussed in the Second Five-year Plan but instead of having a holistic plan for rural housing, piecemeal approach in terms of initiating individual scheme has been adopted. Hence focus of the rural housing should be on the entire village and on habitat improvement through convergence and dovetailing of all the infrastructural services related scheme such as total sanitation campaign. This type strategic intervention can be made only through the Panchayati Raj Institutions.

4. Panchayats in addition to implementing the various central and state sponsored schemes of rural housing, may also develop colonies on their own land situated in the vicinity of the village. For this purpose, they may also mobilize resources from financial institutional to build a affordable appropriate, accessible and acceptable houses on a cost showing basis. In this context example of some villages in Muzaffarnagar District of Uttar Pradesh may be given where some of the innovative farmers having their land in the vicinity of the village have developed that land in to a housing colony. Villagers whose families have expended over a period of time and who have been living in the center of the village purchased the plots with out losing any time.

   In a similar way panchayat have to come forward to initiate such ventures on their land. This short of proposal does have commercial and profit dimension especially in those large villages which are situated on the main roads. For example, there are a number of Gram Panchayats in Haryana whose annual income is running in two lakhs. These panchayats can easily take up such projects. And in case they require additional finance for this purpose, it can be arranged from the financial institution because as per the Panchayat Act, the panchayats have the power to borrow with the previous sanction of the government for carrying out any of the purposes stipulated under the act. The elected representatives of the panchayats should take initiative in this context.

Conclusion

Housing is a basic necessity of the human beings. There is acute shortage of houses in the rural area as is evident from the findings of the 2001 Census. To meet the requirement of houses in the rural areas in addition to Central and State sponsored housing schemes the panchayats themselves should come forward to provide shelter to the villagers in the shortest period. For this purpose, the Panchayats should implement the Centrally-sponsored Schemes in a effective manner by way of activating the GS and selecting only those person who really deserve to have a houses under the IAY. Corruption has to be eliminated from the process of providing houses to the homeless. If this thing is not done at the earliest, people will lose faith in the sanctity of the Institutions of Panchayati Raj and in their social agenda. Hence elected representatives of the panchayat have to be pro-active and careful in this context.

In addition to this panchayats should also take up the work of construction of houses by investing their own resources as well as by borrowing funds for the purpose from financial institution. But this can only happen if the Panchayat leadership realizes the need and work ability of more innovative schemes and takes initiative in this regard.

REFERENCES

Acharya, R.K. 1990: "Problem of Rural Housing", *Indian Journal of Rural Development*.

Basbara, Harriss, 1996: *Panchayati Raj Institution and the Rural Poor*.

Gandhigram Rural Institute, *Village Sanitation*, Faculty of Rural Health and Sanitation, Tamil Nadu.

Rao, Subha, 1998: *Housing for Homeless*.

Parad, J., 1998: *Impact of Regulations of IAY on Rural Sector*.

9

Role of PRIs in Implementing Rural Employment Guarantee Scheme (REGS)

Dr. Sudhansu Se. Nayak* and Dr. Anil Ku. Sahu**

Introduction

The government, as commitment to its national common minimum programme, has successfully passes the bill on National Rural Employment Guarantee Scheme (NREGS) seeking to provide guaranteed employment to at least one member of every rural households for 100 days with a minimum wage of Rs. 60 per day. Now the scheme has the legal force and is to be implemented from the year 2006 in 200 districts. The underlying objective of the scheme has been to ensure food security of rural house holds through providing guaranteed employment which can increase purchasing power of the poor rural families. About 137 million people are expected to benefit under the scheme. Sum of Rs. 17,00,000 million would be spent in the first year covering most vulnerable 200 districts. Then the scheme would be expanded to cover all the districts of the country.

Rural Economic Scenario

Out of 260 million poor people in the country, about 200 million poor people are in rural areas. Around 100 districts are under the constant threat of drought and semi-famine like situation every year. Other 90 districts are facing every year floods and torrential rains.

* Lecturer in Commerce, R.N. College, Dura, Berhampur-10, Ganjam (Orissa).

**Reader in MBA, Berhampur University, Orissa.

While about 25 per cent rural households [landless laborers and bonded labour, have either no income generating assets, 80 per cent farmers being small and marginal have inadequate and/or poor quality of assets with meager or no irrigation facilities. Rural artisans have no access to modern tools/ equipment and marketing. Problem of perpetual and pernicious poverty more particularly in rural areas has been deeply rooted into the large-scale unemployment among rural households during half of the year. Chronic unemployment for a large part of the year is prevalent in hilly, tribal, desert and drought prone areas. The situation become very pathetic when monsoon fails.

According to National Social Watch, 48 per cent people in 13 states of India viz. Andhra Pradesh, Tamil Nadu, Maharashtra, Gujarat, Arunachal Pradesh, Assam, Bihar, Chhattisgarh, Madhya Pradesh, Orissa, Rajasthan and Uttar Pradesh, do not get two meals a day. There are 45 per cent villages in India where people do not work for six months in a year and 20 per cent villages do not have work opportunities for people in any form. Even revamped Public Distribution System does not reach to 68 per cent villages. Food security is a serious problem for poor people in these 13 states. Thus, need for enshrining in our constitution the provision of right of work/employment and food security has very aptly gained tremendous importance in the recent years.

Rural Employment Guarantee Scheme (REGS)

The scheme is meant to provide employment to at least one person for 100 days in a year. During the four months lean period in a year, when agriculture does not provide any work to the rural households, the rural poor would earn additional income of Rs. 6000 in a year. The scheme is, therefore, meant to provide work to these people in their native villages where there is no work for them in agricultural sector. Thus, provision of Rs. 6,000 per person for 100 days that has been guaranteed under the scheme would be an essential component of food security to the family. Besides, there are other government schemes such as, PMGSY under which a sum of Rs. 42,000 million would be spent and implemented in almost every panchayat. There too people would get work/

employment and earn some income for their subsistence, there are other state government sponsored irrigation projects where ponds have to be dug and canals/dams constructed which can also provide employment to rural households and help them earn additional income.

It is essentially a wage employment programme to enable unemployed rural households to earn additional money to guaranteed food security. Second object is to create assets in rural areas. The scheme would employ people in developing infrastructure facilities in villages that would accelerate the process of agricultural and rural development in the country which would improve the quality of life of rural people. Under the scheme economic activities would be undertaken such as, soil and moisture conservation, watershed management, drought and flood proofing, forestry, land development including reclamation of saline/alkaline/degraded land, rural connectivity through arterial roads and the like. All these projects are clearly defined and described in the NREG Act. In addition to this, new projects could also be taken up in some specific areas if the state government feels the need. Watershed development project is significantly important in almost two-thirds districts in India which are drought prone. Watershed management programme to renovate, clean and deepen all old water bodies like ponds, tanks, can very well be undertaken. In this process, groundwater level can be raised that problem of acute drinking water shortages can also be tackled. Similarly, construction of canals and check-dams can improve the irrigation scenario, afforestation can improve water-holding capacity as part of drought and flood proofing programme. This can help horticultural programme to take place in dry-land areas.

Technical experts are carrying out detailed studies and formulating development plans in 150 districts where food-for-work programme will be implemented. Technical experts from AFC, XLRI, IIM and IRMA are drawing plans of individual villages in consultation with local leaders and elected representatives. Comprehensive reports on districts like Aurangabad (Maharashtra), Banswara (Rajasthan) and Banaskantha (Gujarat) are in the advanced stage of formulation. Such reports would be completed for 150 districts and utilized for implementation under the scheme.

Earlier/Existing Programmes

While this scheme has a "human face" and its basic concept has received appreciation from one and all, it should not be out of place if the policy makers learn lessons from the process of planning and implementation of similar schemes/projects on wage employment and asset generation already initiated in past and take corrective measures before implementing this scheme so as to yield expected results. During post-independence era government has recognized the importance of agriculture and improving the quality of rural life and initiated several programmes of which following projects had specific component of rural employment.

1. The self-employment programmes, as an integral part of poverty alleviation, by way of providing subsidy accompanied with bank credit on soft terms to enable rural poor households to purchase/create income generating assets for supplementing their income were introduced from time to time, such as Integrated Rural Development Programme, Development of Women and Children in Rural Areas, Supply of Improved Tool-kits to Rural Artisans and Ganga Kalyan Yojana. The scheme for Training of Rural Youth for Self-employment was also implemented to equip rural youths with necessary skills so as to enhance their capacity to produce/ manufacture quality products of rural/cottage/small/tiny industries in rural areas. These programmes were subsequently merged into a single programme called as "Swarnjayanti Gram Swarozgar Yojana in April, 1991". Assuming that rural poor have abilities and given right type of support they can be successful producers of goods and services, it was, therefore, aimed at establishing a large number of micro-enterprises in the rural areas and building upon the potential of rural poor.

2. Wage employment programme was also introduced undor which poor were provided wage employment on various public works. The Sampoorna Grameen Rozgar Yojana was launched on 25th September 2001 with the

objective of ensuring food security, additional wage employment and creating village infrastructure in rural areas after merging erstwhile Jawahar Gram Samridhi Yojana and Employment Assurance Yojana (JGSY). The JGSY was earlier known as Jawahar Rozgar Yojana which was introduced in 1989 after merging erstwhile National Rural Employment Programme and Rural Landless Employment Guarantee Programme.

3. Special area development programmes were undertaken aiming at creation of infrastructure in the backward areas which also gave employment to marginalized sections of rural areas such as, Drought Prone Areas Programme, Desert Development Programme and Integrated Waste Land Development Programme, Hill Area Development Programme, Hill Area Development Programme, Command Area Development Programme and Integrated Tribal Development Programme.

4. Under Minimum Needs Programme access to basic needs was construed as an integral part of a strategy for eradicating poverty and improving the quality of life of rural population. The conference of Chief Ministers held in 1996 identified seven basic minimum services for the people on priority basis viz. primary health care, universalisation of primary education, safe drinking water, public housing assistance to all shelterless poor families, nutrition, connectivity of all villages and habitations by roads and streaming of the public distribution system with a sharp focus on the poor as the beneficiaries.

These programmes were conceptualized very well to yield specific objectives and results on the target groups of beneficiaries in the concerned geographical areas. However, the objectives achieved and benefits accrued under each of the programmes were not as expected as well as in proportion to the funds invested due to variety of reasons/factors. Most significant reasons can be attributed to utter lack of involvement and participation of local people, for whom these programmes were evolved, in the matter of planning, implementation, monitoring-cum-concurrent evaluation, ex-post impact evaluation and modifying the projects to suit to local conditions and peoples needs. All programmes were planned and implemented by the government officials and through creation of special agencies like District Rural Development Agency etc. rather than involving Panchayati Raj Institutions. Even the worst part in the process of their implementation could be evident from the following observations/studies:

* Our late Prime Minister Rajiv Gandhi once admitted that out of one rupee spent under the government sponsored schemes meant for the economic/social welfare of the people only 15 paise reach to them.
* Recent study of the Rajiv Gandhi Foundation also confirm this statement revealing the fact that the benefits of the Indira Gandhi Avas Yojana have reached to only 15 per cent of intended beneficiaries.
* Under the most popular Maharashtra Employment Guarantee Scheme musters with fictitious names were created which were discovered by the Right to Information Agency.
* Mr. Jean Dreaze, an associate of Nobel Laureate Amartya Sen, has also confirmed that in Madhya Pradesh under similar project on employment generation musters were created indicating payment for 60 days against actual work for three days. He had, also, studies such instances in district of Badwani (MP), Purulia (WB), Sonbara (UP), Surguja (Chhattisgarh), Dungurpur (Rajasthan).
* Family implementation of IRDP throughout the country for a very long period resulted into a loss of enormous amount of bank credit and government subsidy.

Panchayati Raj Institutions

With the passage of 73rd Amendment Act, 1992 (which became law on April 24, 1993), peoples' participation in the process of planning, decision-making, implementation and delivery system in rural India has been recognized. It is therefore, worthy to note that the government is now very keen to involve local people and Panchayati Raj Institutions for implementing this schemed and make them responsible to achieve the underlying objectives. In India rural local government comprises 2,32,278 Village Panchayats, 5,905 Intermediate Panchayats, and 499 District Panchayats, making a total of 2,38,682 at all the three levels. Total number of elected representatives of Panchayats at various levels are 2,92 million of which about one million are women and a large majority of them are first-timers. Impact of the provisions of the 73rd Amendment act concerning reservation for women and disadvantaged sections of the community has been that it has improved women's awareness and perception and had created an urge in them to assert for their rightful share in the decision-making exercise at the local level.

For the first time in the history of post-independence India, Panchayati Raj Institutions are expected to be directly involved in this scheme in such a way that they would implement the scheme as an integral part of rural development plan. Gram Panchayats and Gram Sabhas would decide types of work to be undertaken in the villages and use of funds earmarked under the scheme. Gram Sabha would discuss and approve this plan. Gram Sabhas would also supervise and monitor the implementation of the programme.

While it is laudable that Panchayati Raj Institutions are now roped in the implementation of the scheme which concerns to them it is worthwhile to understand the present status of their functioning and initiating the most desired and essential components viz, participation, empowerment and capacity building of Gram Sabhas and Gram Panchayats through need based training and evolving human resources development policy. Following studies pin-point the immediate need for this:

1. A field-work carried out by the World Bank (2002) in six districts of Rajasthan and Madhya Pradesh to assess to the preparedness of rural constituents to participate in PRIs observed. People participate in the political process but show low level of interest in PRIs as an instrument of democracy and development. People do not participate in the accountability mechanism and in particular the Gram Sabhas which on an average are attended by only seven per cent of eligible population. The explanation for lagging participation is that people perceive little benefit from GPs given

scarce resources under their control. Elected PRIs representatives themselves at every level feel marginalized."

2. Political decentralization does not mean participation only in the electoral process. It calls for active involvement of elected functionaries, Gram Sabhas women and other marginalized groups in the functioning of rural local self-government institutions and pursuit of collective decision-making process, and their own systems of accountability, responsiveness and transparent governance.
3. Effective planning at the grassroots level can only be envisioned if a large number of GS members actively participate in the planning process. At present 50 per cent members (women) are virtually outside the GS meetings because they are not allowed to participate by their male family members and another big chunk mostly SC/ST and other weaker sections do not attend due to some compulsions. These members are less motivated to attend meetings because they do not expect any gain from such meetings but lose their one-day wage.

No doubt, 73rd Amendment Act has given a new role and responsibility to the PRIs in India. However, the most crucial and significant drawback/deficiency in the act has been that, the functions and powers of PRIs have been left to the discretion of the State Governments, instead of having been clearly specified and defined. In fact the Article 243G should have been like this "the legislature of a state should, by law, endow the panchayat with such powers and authority as shall be necessary to enable them to function as institution of self-government and should contain provisions for the devolution of powers and responsibilities upon panchayats at the appropriate level with respect to:

(1) the preparation of plans for economic development and social justice, and

(2) the implementation of schemes for economic development and social justice as may be entrusted to them including those in relation to the matters listed

in the 11th Schedule. Thus, the Article 243G of the constitution should have envisaged Panchayats as "institutions of self-government" and should have given full functional, financial and administrative autonomy in their working.

Participation and Empowerment

Participation is an active process by which beneficiaries acquire knowledge, understand role, responsibilities and functions of the concerned institutions including their own, influence the direction and execution of a development project so as to ensure their well-being in terms of income, personal growth, self-reliance or other values which the projects underline as the objectives. It is, therefore, absolutely essential that not only the likely beneficiaries under the NREGS but also all the rural households of the village must participate to secure all the details of the scheme, its short and long-term advantages and disadvantages as also the precise role and responsibilities of all the concerned individuals, Gram Sabha, Gram Panchayat, beneficiary - households and government officials in planning and implementing and monitoring its progress as well as evaluating the impact of the scheme on the beneficiaries. This should enable the Gram Sabha in particular and Gram Panchayat in general to put all their efforts to make the scheme a success in achieving its objectives viz, guaranteed employment and additional income in a very much transparent manner, food security and overall development of the village infrastructure and economy in the years to come.

The process of empowerment is both individual and collective, since it is through involvement in groups that people most often begin to become aware and develop the ability to organize themselves for taking decision in bringing about change.

Empowerment is a multifaceted process which calls for pooling of resources to secure collective strength and countervailing power, and entail the improvement of manual and technical skills; administrative and managerial capabilities, and planning and analytical abilities of local people. Empowerment of Gram Sabha in particular must transfer these skills, capabilities and abilities to the village people and facilitate them to plan for the smooth implementation of the scheme taking into account the availability of financial resources and technical inputs; supervise the execution of various components of the NREG scheme; identify the constraints inhibiting its implementation and initiate measures to modify the planning process and its implementation etc.

Capacity Building

PRIs knowledge, skills, and capabilities need to be substantially improved in order to resolve the problems coming in the way of fiscal and administrative decentralization. For this purpose, suitable capacity building measures need to be adopted so that finance, functions and functionaries are transferred smoothly. Capacity building may be defined as support or intervention that empowers Gram Sabha and Gram Panchayat as organization to achieve the objectives underlying the scheme. Effective capacity building requires the interaction of learning-by-doing, access to resources, facilitation, mediation and training.

Capacity building measures for Gram Sabhas consist of creation of enabling environment with appropriate policy and legal frameworks; institution building; human resource development and strengthening of managerial capability. Capacity building measures also refer to developing community audit skills, formulating common vision, demonstrating the importance of setting and prioritizing realistic objectives consistent with local values, facilitating a strategic plan and phased operational measures and encouraging the monitoring and evaluation of progress. Under the NREG Scheme the capacity building should result into:

1. Effective participation of all rural households, more importantly women and other marginalized groups in Gram Sabha meetings and discussion leading to decision-making process.
2. Elimination of caste, class and gender divide in the constitution of Gram Panchayat.
3. Evolution of result-oriented plan of activities, strategic execution and monitoring system in line with the objectives of the NREG Scheme.

4. Efficient mobilization of local resources (physical, natural and human) for the development of village economy.
5. Better understanding of local self-governance and democratic values while taking decision.
6. Effective coordination and communication between Gram Panchayat and Gram Sabha to resolve problems and avoid misunderstanding/communication gap.
7. Better networking and coordination between voluntary organizations and the Gram Sabhas/Gram Panchayat to share experiences for mutual benefits.
8. Effective delivery of development programme leading to achieving the expected objectives/results.
9. Adequate transparency in respect of scheme implementation including selection of targeted beneficiary, use of funds/resources and accountability of planners and implementers to Gram Sabhas.

Need For

For the emergence of Gram Sabha as a body to whom the Gram Panchayat is accountable there is need to spell out the powers and functions of Gram Sabha in great detail, articulating its role as planner, decision-maker and auditor. Further a massive awareness creation programme is required to inform Gram Sabha and Gram Panchayat about its role in planning, implementation, managing financial resources, accounting and audit of the NREG scheme and accountability to achieve objectives of the scheme. In this context following measures need immediate attention.

1. Since the NREG scheme has been extremely important and calls for significant involvement of local people and PRIs more particularly Gram Sabha and Gram Panchayat right from the stage of planning it is absolutely essential to impart comprehensive training for transferring various skills. For this purpose it would be necessary to assign the role to National Institute of Rural Development to design training syllabus focusing sharply on all aspects of planning, implementing, managing financial resources, account-

ing, audit, monitoring-cum-concurrent evaluation and ex-post impact evaluation etc. for both the Gram Sabha and Gram Panchayat. Training based on this syllabus must be imparted at block level by State Rural Development Institutes on a planner and war footing basis. Besides, it is necessary to organize Workshop on Implementation of NREG scheme at block levels for two days for the benefit of Gram Panchayats and selected members of GS which an identify critical issues for Gram Sabha and Gram Panchayat during the process of planning to impact evaluation and the support (technical, financial and administrative) required by them from block/district/state/union Government with the ultimate objective of making the scheme implementation by PRIs a success.

2. As involvement of PRIs under this scheme is a beginning endeavors must be made to train PRIs in all aspects of implementing schemes of farm and rural development in near future. For this purpose process of formulating block level plans and positioning planning machinery at district level as recommended by the Dantwala Committee in 1978 should be initiated. While formulating block level plans all infrastructure facilities pointed out by District Development Managers of NABARD may need to be included.

3. Information Technology intervention is necessary to create data base as well as ensuring transparency and probity by exhibiting the transactions. Progress of work, future plans and actions and thereby allowing access of the GS; increasing the effectiveness and efficiency of services provided by various agencies and enhancing coordination within the different segments of the functional departments etc.

4. Monitoring-cum-concurrent evaluation of the scheme on a regular and continuing basis should be entrusted to independent professional institutions and deficiencies noticed must be corrected on time.

5. Review and monitoring of the implementation progress may need to be done on a monthly basis at PRI level. It should also be done quarterly at the State level and

half yearly at the national level by a High Power Committee chaired by the cabinet Minister for Rural Development concerned. Factors inhibiting progress and deficiencies pointed out by monitoring-cum-concurrent evaluation authority should resolved through policy changes, if need be.

6. Minister for Rural Development must brief on a half yearly basis MPs attached to his/her Ministry and make a detailed presentation in the parliament on a half yearly basis.
7. Local and national print and electronic media may consider necessary to release full report on a quarterly basis giving scope for constructive criticism.
8. Current year's implementation in 200 districts would provide feedback and experiences which may be written as case studies by Management experts to improve future policy and strategy in its implementation.

Conclusion

This scheme is unique in its concept and implementation and, therefore, role of PRIs, State and Union Government needs to be well defined to avoid ambiguity and make each institution accountable in respect of achieving the objectives of the scheme. In this process comprehensive training syllabus, plan and programme must be designed for GS and GP and its implementation must be monitored at higher level.

REFERENCES

Districts at a Glance, 2006, Government of Orissa, Bhubaneswar.

Economic Survey, 2006-06, Government of Orissa, Bhubaneswar.

Kurukshetra, Vol. 53, No.7, May 2005 & Vol. 54, No. 10 August 2006.

NREGA 2005, operational guidelines, Ministry of Rural Development, Government of India.

Orissa REGS 2005 Draft.

Souvenir on NREGS, 2005, Utkal University, Vani Vihar, Orissa.

Statistical Abstracts, 2005, Government of Orissa, Bhubaneswar.

The Gazette of India (Extraordinary), No. 48, New Delhi, Sept. 7, 2005.

Yojana, Vol. 48, No. 7, May 2004 & Vol. 50, March 2006.

10

Orissa Grama Panchayat Act: A Milestone for Family Discipline

Surendra Nath Panda*

Discipline is the way of life. Unless we are disciplined, we cannot achieve success. Though it can be practised in life, still the circumstances in which we survive, also play major role towards establishment of this factor. Different enactments have also been framed to achieve this goal. One of such enactment is Orissa Gram Panchayat Act. Though this act tells us regarding the qualifications and disqualifications to be a member of the Gram Panchayat, still it assures us the way of discipline.

Soon after enforcement of our constitution, we have adopted democratic form of bodies from the remote village to till the apex unit, Orissa Grama Panchayat Act has also adopted democratic form of units. This act prescribes qualifications and disqualifications in its different chapters and rules. Section 11 of the Orissa Grama Panchayat Act prescribes qualifications for Membership in the Gram Panchayat. No member of a Grama Sasan shall be eligible to stand for election.

Section 11

(a) as a *sarpanch* if he –

(1) is a candidate for election as a member of the Grama Panchayat in respect of any ward; or

(2) xxx xxx xxx

(3) is a candidate for election or holds office as a sarpanch of any other Grama Panchayat;

* Advocate, Aska, Ganjam, Orissa.

(b) as a *sarpanch* or *naib-sarpanch*, if he has not attained the age of 21 years or is unable to read and write Oriya;

(c) as a member-

(1) for more than one ward in the Grama or for more than one Grama Panchayat; or

(2) if he is unable to read and write Oriya; and

(3) if he has not attained the age of twenty-one years.

Similarly Section 25 of the Orissa Grama Panchayat Act prescribes disqualification for Membership of Grama Panchayat. There are some provisions for disqualification in Section 25. Out of those provisions, the following provisions are very much important as it ensures discipline in family life.

Section 25

(1) A person shall be disqualified for being elected or nominated as, a sarpanch or any other member of the Gram Panchayat constituted under this Act, if he-

××× ××× ×××

(u) has more than one spouse living; or

(v) has more than two children:

Provided that the disqualification under Clause (v) shall not apply to any person who has more than two children on the date of commencement of the Orissa Grama Panchayats (Amendment) Act, 1994 or, as the case may be, within a period of one year of such commencement, unless he begets an additional child after the said period of one year.

Hindu Marriage Act of 1955 has prescribed monogamy. Basing on the principle of Hindu Marriage Act, Orissa Grama Panchayat Act has also been shaped. It also prescribed one living spouse. Orissa Grama Panchayat Act has also framed rules for registrations of marriages. Rule 73 of Orissa Grama Panchayat Rules prescribes provisions for registration of births, deaths, marriages, etc. and the rule is as follows:

All births, deaths, marriages and epidemic diseases occurring in the villages within the grama shall be registered and reported to the prescribed authorities in the matter as specified in the following rules. The Grama Panchayat may appoint a member of the ward or the Grama Panchayat Secretary or any other persons as Recorder. The recorder after receiving information on births, deaths, marriages and epidemic diseases occurring in the villages, shall enter them in relevant registers and communicate the same to the Grama Panchayat.

Section 8 of Hindu Marriage Act prescribes registration of Hindu marriages, adopting the same principle, Orissa Grama Panchayat Act has also prescribes similar rules as mentioned above. Registration of marriages has a very good affect not only for the family but also for the society as a whole. The Apex Court of our land while dealing a writ petition in between *Smt. Seema* Vrs. *Ashwani Kumar* reported in 2006 (1) OLR (SC) 299 has observed registration of marriage as an important factor. The said observation is as follows:

> . . . if the marriage is registered it also provided evidence of the marriage having taken place and it would provide a rebuttable presumption of the marriage having taken place. Though, the registration itself can not be a proof of valid marriage *per se*, and would not be the determinative factor regarding validity of a marriage, yet it has a great evidentiary value in the matters of custody of children, right of the children born from the wedlock of the two persons whose marriage is registered and the age of parties to the marriage. That being so, it would be in the interest of the society if marriages are made compulsory registrable. The legislative intent of enacting Section 8 of the Hindu Marriage Act is apparent from the use of the expression for the purpose of facilitating the proof of Hindu marriages.

In another landmark decision our Apex Court while dealing a Writ Petition in respect of an inter-caste marriage between *Lata Singh* Vrs. *State of U.P. and another* published in 2006 (II) OLR (SC) 502 has given the following observation regarding the institution of marriage.

The caste system is a curse on the nation and the sooner it is destroyed the better. In fact, it is dividing the nation at a time when we have to be united to face the challenges before the nation unitedly. Hence, inter-caste marriages are in fact in the national interest as they will result in destroying the caste system. However, disturbing news is coming from several parts of the country that young men and women, who undergo inter-caste marriage, are threatened with violence, or violence is actually committed on them. In our opinion, such acts of violence or threats or harassment are wholly illegal and those who commit them must be severely punished. This is a free and democratic country, and once a person becomes a major he or she can marry whosoever he/she likes. If the parents of the boy or girl do not approve of such inter-caste or inter-religious marriage the maximum they can do is that they can cut off social relations with the son or the daughter, but they can not give threats or commit or instigate acts of violence and cannot harass the person who undergoes such inter-caste or inter-religious marriage. We therefore, direct that the administration/police authorities throughout the country will see to it that if any boy or girl who is a major undergoes inter-caste or inter-religious marriage with a woman or man who is a major. The couple are not harassed by anyone nor subjected to threats or acts of violence and anyone who gives threats or harasses are commits act of violence either himself or at his instigation is taken to task by instigating criminal proceedings by the police against such persons and further stern action is taken against such persons as provided by law.

So from the two landmark decisions of the Apex Court as described above we come to the conclusion that the institution of marriage is an important factor. Orissa Gram Panchayat Act has also given similar importance to the institution of marriage, as it prescribes monogamy and two child norm systems. Hence, Orissa Grama Panchayat Act is a milestone which ensures family discipline. Unless the member obliges the provisions then he/she will be ousted from the post.

REFERENCES

Desai, S.T., *Hindu Marriage Act, Principles of Hindu Law*, N.M. Tripathy Pvt. Ltd., Bombay, 1990.

Panchayat Laws in Orissa, *Orissa Law Reviews* (OLR), Cuttack, 2002, pp. 14, 23, 112.

11

Peoples Participation in Panchayati Raj Governance through Gram Sabha

Bhagaban Padhy*

Panchayati Raj Institutions (PRIs) were not new in Indian soil. These institutions were found even in vedic and pre-vedic periods. These institutions were strengthened at the governmental level during the period of Lord Rippon. It was also a long cherished dream of Gandhiji to make villages economically self-sufficient and politically sound through *gram swaraj*.

Gandhiji's idea of "*gram swaraj*" was rightly felt by the Constituent Assembly and necessary provisions were made in the Article 40 of Directive Principles of State Policy (DPSP) under Art. IV of the Constitution. It reads as, "the state shall take steps to organize Village Panchayat and endow them with such powers and authority as may be necessary to enable them to function as units of self government" with a view to strengthen the PR institutes different committees have been constituted by the Government of India from time to time. These are the Balwant Ray Mehta Committee (1957), Ashok Mehta Committee (1977), Committee headed by G.K.V. Rao (1986), committee under the chairmanship of L.M. Singvi and a sub-committee under the chairmanship of Mr. P.K. Thungon.

On the basis of the recommendations of P.K. Thungon Committee 73rd and 74th Amendments were made to Indian Constitution to ensure more constitutional powers to Village Panchayats and local urban bodies. The 73rd Amendment deals

* Lecturer in Economics of A.N. College, Dharakote, Ganjam, Orissa.

with Villages Panchayats and 74th Amendment deals with urban local bodies 73rd Amendment provides vide ranging powers to Gram Sabha which is the core of the panchayat system and extends ample scopes for all eligible voters.

Grama Sabha and its Functions

1. There shall be at least two meetings one in February and the other in June every year of the members of the Grama Sasan and such other meetings as may be prescribed.
2. (a) The quorum for the meetings of the Grama Sasan (hereinafter referred to as the "Grama Sabha") shall be one-tenth of the members of the Grama Sasan.

   (b) in the event of there being no quorum at any Grama Sabha it shall stand adjourned to a future day of which notice shall be given in the prescribed manner and no quorum shall be necessary for any such adjourned meeting.

   (c) Subject to the other provisions of this act, it shall be the duty of the Grama Sasan to consider:

   (i) at the Grama Sabha held in February each year, the programmes and works to be under taken by the Grama Panchayat for the ensuing year and the annual budget for the *grama* for that year having regard to the recommendation, if any of the different *palli sabha* with the *grama* made in accordance with the provisions of Section 6 and give its recommendations to the Grama Panchayat;

   (ii) at the Grama Sabha held during the month of June each year, the report of the programmes and works undertaken by the Grama Panchayat and their progress during the preceding year along with the annual audit report submitted by the *sarpanch*;

   (iii) at any Grama Sabha, proposals for levy of taxes, rates, rents and fees and the enhance-ment of rates thereof; organisation of community service, drawing up and implementation of agricultural production plans and any other matter as may be prescribed; and,

(iv) the implementation of revised budget, if any, for the Grama made under sub-section (2) of section 98 and give its recommendation to the Grama Panchayat.

3. Subject to the provisions of Sub-section (1) the meetings of the Grama sasan shall be convened by such authority, in such a manner and at such time and intervals as may be prescribed.
4. The business of Grama Sasan at the Grama Sabha shall be conducted and the record of the proceedings thereof shall be maintained in the prescribed manner.

In a nutshell Gram Sabha is expected to deliver the functions such as:

1. To strengthen democracy at the grass root level.
2. To lavy foundation of Panchayati Raj setup.
3. To control over panchayats.
4. To create better community harmony.
5. To establish effective communication.
6. To act as an agency of social and political education,
7. To control over village level functionaries.
8. To act as a grass root agency for planning and development.
9. To establish democratic supervision.

In this back drop attempts have been made in this research write up to explore the following objectives:

1. To highlight role and functions of Gram Sabha in the state of Orissa.
2. To make a case study of Dharakote Panchayat samiti, and members of Gram Sabha of two gram panchayats named Jahada and Saba.
3. To know about the constraints faced by Gram Sabha members.
4. Concluding remarks.

Methodology

Keeping in view the objectives of the study, Panchayat Samiti, Dharakote in the district of Ganjan (Orissa) has been selected purposively for its quite uneven growth and development and high tribal concentration. The area of study covers only two Gram Panchayats out of 17 functioning under Dharakote Panchayat Samiti.

Data have been collected both from primary and secondary sources in order to know about the working and functioning of Gram Panchayats and Gram Sabhas. To analyse the above facts 60 Gram Sabha members (30 from each G.P.) have been interviewed and selection of the respondents was made on the basis of simple random sampling method. Gram Panchayats selected for the study are Jahada and Saba problems enquiry schedules have been prepared in order to know the awareness of Gram Sabha members. For the collection of primary data questionnaire method by the help of personal interview have been adopted. For the secondary data official records magazines, journals have been taken resort to percentage method has been followed to infer conclusion.

Table 1
Representation of different groups in Gram Sabha

Group	*Yes*	*No*	*Not Necessary*	*Total (%)*
Higher caste	05 (08.3)	08 (13.3)	47 (78.3)	60 (100.0)
Educated people	51 (85.0)	02 (03.3)	07 (11.7)	60 (100.0)
Rich people	03 (05.0)	10 (16.7)	47 (78.3)	60 (100.0)
Male as compared to female	12 (20.0)	06 (10.0)	42 (70.0)	60 (100.0)
Politically active	23 (38.3)	09 (15.0)	28 (46.7)	60 (100.0)
Religious person	20 (33.3)	08 (13.3)	32 (53.3)	60 (100.0)
Government employee	18 (30.0)	07 (11.7)	35 (58.3)	60 (100.0)
People with village	54 (90.0)	01 (01.7)	05 (08.3)	60 (100.0)
Development attitude Local leader	47(78.3)	04(06.7)	09(15.0)	60(100.0)

Opinion was sought about the representation of different groups in panchayat for better performance. Opinion regarding higher caste for better performance is yes (8.3%), no (13.3%), not necessary (78.3%). Opinion regarding educated people for better performance is yes (85.0%), no (3.3%), not necessary (11.7%). Opinion regarding rich people for better performance is yes (5.0%), no (16.7%), not necessary (78.3%). Opinion regarding male as compared to female for better performance is yes (20.0%), no (10.0%), not necessary (70.0%). Opinion regarding politically active people for better performance is yes (38.3%), no (15.0%), not necessary (46.7%). Opinion regarding religious persons for better performance is yes (33.3%), no (13.3%), not necessary (53.3%). Opinion regarding government employee for better performance is yes (30.0%), no (11.7%), not necessary (58.3%). Opinion regarding people having village development orientaitons for bettr performance is yes (90.0%), no (1.7%), not necessary (8.3%). Opinion regarding local leader for better performance is yes (78.3%), no (6.7%), not necessary (15.0%).

The above analysis clearly depicts that people having village development orientations, educated people and local leaders are considered good for better performance of panchayats. This demonstrates that at local level conceptually the respondents agree to have better leadership.

Table 2
Dominance in Panchayat/Gram Sabha

Sl. No.	*Category*	*Number of respondents*	*Percentage*
1.	Sarapanch	09	15.0
2.	Socio-economic elite	01	01.7
3.	Higher caste people	01	01.7
4.	Educated people	03	05.0
5.	Anti-socio elements	06	10.0
6.	Don't Know	01	01.7
7.	Nobody	39	65.0
	Total	60	100.0

Sixty-five per cent respondents are of the view that nobody dominated the panchayat/Gram Sabha. Fifteen per cent respondnets point out that sarapanch dominates the panchayat/

Gram Sabha. Ten per cent respondents express the view that panchayat/Gram Sabha is dominated by anti social elements. 5.0 per cent respondents say that people dominate panchayat/ Gram Sabha. One respondent each points out that panchayat/ Gram Sabha is dominated by local-economic elites and higher caste people whereas remaining one respondent does not know about this problem.

The above analysis clearly depicts that almost two-third respondents feel that nobody dominated panchayat/Gram Sabha. It is indeed a positive and encouraging sign that respondents do not have the feeling that there is any domination either of a person or of any outside agency. Of course, sarpanch and anti-social elements have been referred as dominant groups that should be a real cause for worry for the panchayat/Gram Sabha.

It is a evident from Table 3 that highly educated people are more aware of Grama Sabha when compared to less educated. Employees either private or government are more aware of Grama Sabha when compared to other categories of people. Finally, it can be concluded that educaiton and employment are the important factor to determine the level of awareness about grama sabha and its functioning which ultimately leads to better functioning of Grama Sabha as well as better management of gram panchayat resources for speedy village development.

Shortcomings/Constraints

1. The privileged class which gains the upper hand in these institutions spoils the entire process in attaining the goal.
2. Involvement of politicians/supporters of the local block chairman/MLA/Samiti Member/Sarpanch/confines the programme to limited and vested interest groups.
3. Under the table deal between the B.D.O. and favoured contractors is another problem area in the proper implementation of different scheme through Gram Sabha favoured contractor.
4. Dominant role played by the minority i.e. landlords, or powerful moneylenders. These persons dominate the

Table 3
Awareness among People about Gram Sabha and its Functioning

Particulars		*No. of Times attended Gram Sabha*					
		1-5 times		*6-10 times*		*11 times & above*	
		Count	*Raw%*	*Count*	*Raw%*	*Count*	*Raw%*
Literacy of the Respondents	Illiterate	9	29.0%	7	22.6%	1	3.2%
	Primary	6	13.0%	11	23.9%	6	13.0%
	High School	14	12.6%	23	20.7%	11	9.9%
	College	33	21.4%	23	14.9%	32	20.8%
Occupation of the Respondents	Agriculture Labourer	6	14.0%	11	25.6%	5	11.6%
	Farmer	16	15.8%	21	20.8%	22	21.8%
	Govt. Employee	13	16.7%	12	15.4%	10	12.8%
	Private Employee	17	17.5%	17	17.5%	8	8.2%
	Self Employment	4	30.8%	2	15.4%	5	38.5%
	Allied Activities	6	60.0%	1	10.0%	0	0.00%

Age of the Respondents	Below 25	2	25.5%	1	12.5%	3	37.5%
	26 - 35	4	7.4%	15	27.8%	12	22.2%
	36 - 45	20	16.5%	25	20.7%	13	10.7%
	46 - 55	28	25.5%	15	13.6%	12	10.9%
	56 and above	8	16.3%	8	16.3%	10	20.4%
Annual Income of the Respondents	Below 10,000	13	17.9%	21	25.6%	15	18.3%
	10,001-20,000	16	15.2%	22	21.0%	22	21.0%
	20,001-50,000	18	20.7%	9	10.3%	10	11.5%
	50,001-1,00,000	10	17.9%	11	19.6%	3	5.4%
	1,00,001 and above	5	21.7%	1	8.3%	0	0.0%

entire village atmosphere and in most of the cases their authority is not questioned by the poor villagers.

5. The illiterate and ignorant villagers are unable to take active interest in the formulation or execution of the plans for the development of local areas.
6. In the countryside today we find different groups with varying interest which proves as a hurdle in the way of smooth functioning of these institutions.
7. The interference of the government officials either directly or indirectly is the most dangerous thing for the full and unfettered performance of these institutions.

Causes of Failure

The following are the reasons of failure of Gram Sabha:

1. Lack of political will

The basic reason for the decay of Gram Sabha is the negative role of political leaders. This is because they hesitate to hand over the real power directly to the people.

2. Lack of sufficient powers.

Gram Sabha has not been vested with sufficient powers. It has no effective decision making power.

3. Lack of faith

Politicians, administrations, village level functionaries and even the people have not much faith in the working of Gram sabha. Thus, the collapse of Gram Favoured contractor is not a matter of surprise.

4. Failure of Panchayati Raj System

The failure of panchayati Raj system itself is a cause of decay of all the institutions involved in it.

5. Lack of provision

In several states, the respective panchayati Raj Acts were/are silent about the institution of Gram Sabha. Though, in some states, there has been a provision of Gram sabha, yet it has not been strong enough to strengthen this basic institution.

Suggestions for Success and Concluding Remarks

In order to make the Gram Sabha a grand success, I extend my support to the suggestions made in the Diwakar Committee report which are discussed below:

1) Gram Sabha should be statutorily recognized in each state and its meetings should be held more frequently.
2) The meetings of the Gram Sabha should be held by situation in each of the constituent village.
3) In the meetings of the Gram Sabha, decision making as for as possible be achieved through arriving at consensus.
4) Panchayat should be composed of elected members and all adult members of the area should elect the sarapanch.
5) State Govermnet should explore the possibility of appointing a Panchayati Raj Court.
6) Gram sabha should be fully associated with the implementation of village production plans.
7) Having regard to the considerations of liability and community characteristics a population of about 400 to 500 should have a Gram Sabha.

Index